THIRTY YEARS
AT
BRICKLAYERS ARMS

Southern steam from the footplate

by

Michael Jackman

DAVID & CHARLES: NEWTON ABBOT LONDON
NORTH POMFRET (VT) VANCOUVER

ISBN 0 7153 7186 X

Library of Congress Catalog Card Number
75-31329

Set in 11 on 13pt Linotype Baskerville
and printed in Great Britain by
Latimer Trend & Company Ltd Plymouth
for David & Charles (Publishers) Limited
Brunel House   Newton Abbot   Devon

Published in the United States of America
by David & Charles Inc
North Pomfret   Vermont 05053   USA

Published in Canada
by Douglas David & Charles Limited
1875 Welch Street   North Vancouver   BC

Contents

Bricklayers Arms in the 1930s

In 1930, Bricklayers Arms Motive Power Depot had been in operation for just 86 years. Situated at the northern end of the Old Kent Road, close to London Bridge, the depot provided the motive power for many of the Dover, Ramsgate and Hastings trains in and out of Charing Cross and Cannon Street stations. It also coaled, watered and turned visiting engines from Ramsgate, Deal, Dover and St Leonards sheds and when necessary carried out urgent repairs to visiting engines, as well as its own, by its capable staff of fitters. It was first and foremost a South Eastern shed, serving the former SER routes that had become part of the Southern Railway Eastern Section. Its activities on the Brighton line and former LBSCR routes forming the Central Section only came later after the closure of New Cross Gate shed in 1947. The area is steeped in railway history, for this was the territory of the London & Greenwich Railway, the first steam commercial passenger railway in London, opened in 1836.

In many aspects of railway working nicknames or pet names, some of which become semi-official from common usage, were applied to particular locations, depots, sidings and the like, the origins of which sometimes were lost in antiquity. Others were merely abbreviations, and to generations of enginemen Bricklayers Arms was always known as 'B Arms' or just 'The Brick'.

The 30 years of steam working at Bricklayers Arms described in these pages cover probably the most interesting period in its history, for while the Southern electric system was gradually expanding from its mid-1920s inauguration in the South-East London suburbs to its culmination with electrification of the main line routes to Dover in 1959/62, the Southern introduced new express steam locomotive designs which could compare favourably with anything turned out by the other three group companies for similar work. Yet almost to the end of steam one could still see in the late 1950s some of the pre-grouping locomotive survivals steadily coping from time to time in Kent and Sussex with secondary services, even on rare occasions as substitutes for a failed locomotive on top class work. What one did not see from the train or the lineside was the battle on the footplate to keep up steam pressure with an engine not in the best of condition, and part of a fleet being run down for scrapping. The shed fitters played their part in keeping the older engines on the road but with diesels and electrics hoving in sight stocks of spares were often non-existent near the end.

Bricklayers Arms consisted of three engine sheds—the Old Shed, the Carriage or St Patrick's shed, and the New Shed. The Old Shed was part of the first engine shelter built there in 1844, though by 1931 it was twice the original size. The Carriage Shed was so called since carriages used to be berthed there until Bricklayers Arms station closed to the general public in 1852. How this shed came to be known alternatively as St Patrick's no one could explain. The New Shed was, not surprisingly, the last shed erected there and was situated at right-angles to the other sheds on the far side of the turntable. The accompanying plan shows that Bricklayers Arms was a large, sprawling place, the entrance and exit to which was through the large goods depot of the same name, with a railway policeman at the gate adjacent to Pages Walk, which led directly into the Old Kent Road.

For locomotives proceeding to the three nearby terminal stations of London Bridge, Cannon Street or Charing Cross, their route took them past Willow Walk goods sheds—part of the Central or ex-Brighton Section, past Sorting Sidings, Mercer's Crossing and to Rotherhithe Road, where much of the spare coaching stock was stabled. The locomotives then climbed uphill to North Kent East signalbox, where they

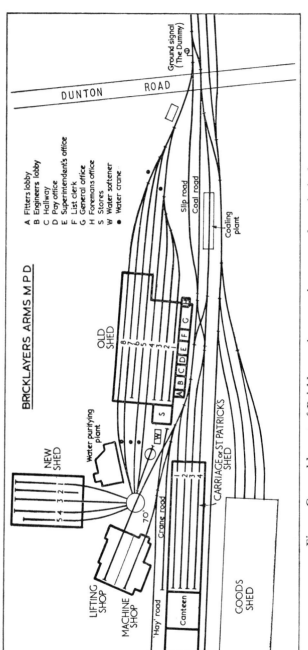

Fig 1   General layout of Bricklayers Arms motive power depot in its last years

ventured on to the main running lines, reversed, and ran up to London Bridge or beyond. It was an inconvenient route to say the least.

The limits of the depot extended to Dunton Road Bridge, on the far side of which was a small ground signal (known forever as 'the Dummy') which governed the entry to the Bricklayers Arms Branch. Engines entering the depot did so by means of a calling-on signal, situated at the country end of Dunton Road bridge.

Engines approached Bricklayers Arms Loco from New Cross Gate by way of Bricklayers Arms Junction and then down to a signal close by a pyjama factory. Engines coming from North Kent West were given a shunt signal, situated on the gantry carrying the North Kent West Home signal, which allowed them to proceed as far as Rotherhithe Road Box. The usual method of entry was by calling-on signals for the journey up the branch, which allowed a number of light engines to follow one another, at a respectful distance, into the Depot proper.

In the early 1930s, the large number of men unemployed kept industrial disputes to a minimum, since there were many willing hands to take the chance of any work—at almost any rate of pay. Bricklayers Arms had never been an easy depot to manage, but the governor in charge at that time was a terror. George Oxley was his name, and such was his powerful character, that men still spoke of him in awe some 25 years later—a tribute that would have pleased Mr Oxley had he been alive to hear it.

George Oxley became known at B Arms—and other depots on the Eastern Section—as 'the man of three words'. It was the practice of men starting a day's work to collect from the time clerk a leaden disc, stamped with the pay number of the employee. Once the disc was taken from its rack, the holder was booked on duty and similarly when the disc or 'lead' was dropped into a slot in the office wall, the time of so doing was entered in the daily pay book. Oxley's rule of iron allowed no complaints, lateness, or incivility, let alone

8

smoking in the sheds or on the footplate. Infringement of his many rules was punished simply by a crisp order 'Drop your lead' to the offender and thereby losing the rest of the day's work—and pay. He had the uncanny habit of appearing when least expected in the most unexpected places, be it inside a firebox being re-stayed or in the disposal areas. His apparent ability to walk straight to a spot where some irregularity was taking place kept everyone, from the newest cleaner to the oldest driver, in a state of toil, which was the whole idea. Every B Arms engine was cleaned to perfection and Oxley would walk round the many locomotives in his care, at all hours of the day and night, to ensure that every cleaner used as much elbow grease as he was capable of producing—and a bit more. Like many hard task-masters, though, Oxley would never hear a word against any of 'his men at B Arms' from an outsider.

Bricklayers Arms depot duties for men and engines, like all steam locomotive depots up and down the country, were divided into 'links', each link covering groups of trains with an allocation of men qualified for the type of duty and locomotives suitable for the work. The links were organised broadly on the type of trains to be covered and ranged from shunting turns, freight and local passenger turns to the links covering the principal expresses. Progress through the links was by seniority so that a man might be a driver for many years before he reached the top link.

The top link engines at the depot were the L1 class inside-cylinder 4-4-os built new as a Maunsell development of the SECR L class 4-4-os. The latter were known as the 'Germans' for a batch was built by Borsig of Berlin just before the outbreak of the first world war. With Deal shed, B Arms had the responsibility of running the 80 minute 'Folkestone Flyers'; starting from Charing Cross, calling at Waterloo and then fast to Folkestone in 80min, these crack expresses were an exacting duty, and the fitting staff saw to it that the engines allocated were in top class condition in every way. Sharing duties in the No 1 and No 2 links with the L1s were the L

9

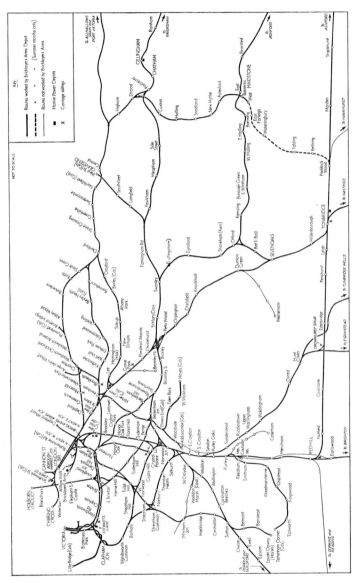

Fig 2 London area routes worked by Bricklayers Arms men and engines

class engines. With the introduction of the heavier Maunsell corridor coaches, train weights were approaching the limit of capacity for the Germans and the rebuilt versions of the earlier SECR 4–4–0s of classes D and E (usually known as 'coppertops' because of their former polished domes) classified as D1 and E1.

The most difficult route was the Hastings run, with its long climbs and twisting curves, many of which, because of their small radius, were checkrailed, adding to the collar work by friction. The Southern Railway was well aware that a more powerful type of locomotive was needed on the Hastings run and Maunsell had prepared a modified, shorter, 4–4–0 version of the Lord Nelson class 4–6–0 to cover this much needed requirement. The SEC route to Hastings, moreover, included a number of tunnels whose clearances were never as generous as elsewhere, and, with tracks through them slightly closer than standard, have limited the width of engines and coaches to about 8ft or so depending on the length and over-hang on curves. This mattered little in pre-grouping days because practically all SECR engines and stock were within this width. By the 1920s, when new designs were being built to the full width of 9ft permitted by the loading gauge on most other routes, the restrictions of the Hastings line called for specially-designed motive power and stock which has applied right down to today with 'Hastings gauge' diesel trains and locomotives. The new 4–4–0s of the late 1920s were intended specifically for the Hastings line although at various times they have been allocated to other parts of the SR and of course were used on other Kent and Sussex lines as part and parcel of their workings on the Hastings line. The Southern Railway, conscious of the publicity value of naming engines, decided to call the new engines after notable schools and thus was born the Schools class.

Much has been written about the Schools and a repetition of their design evolution and development is unnecessary in this book, but the performance and reliability of these remarkable engines made them a legend in their own time

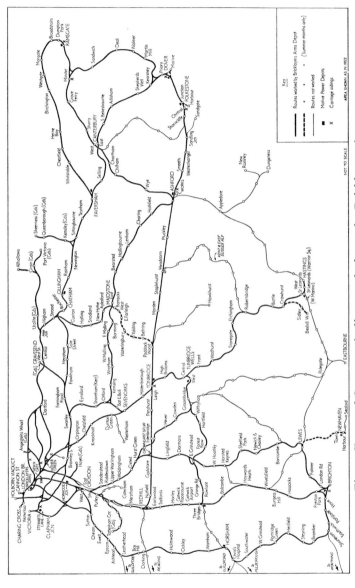

Fig 3   Kent and Sussex main lines worked over by Bricklayers Arms crews

and no man who has had the privilege to work on them will ever forget them. That they were to remain top link engines at Bricklayers Arms, St Leonards, Dover, and Ramsgate sheds until the end of steam operation was proof enough of their reliability.

Due to much engineering work having to be completed on the Hastings line, the first Schools 4–4–0s went to the Western Section, but by the end of 1931, B Arms men had made the acquaintance of the Schools class and from then on the engines were firm favourites. The first inkling that they were out of the ordinary was on the race-track between Tonbridge and Ashford—that superb, almost level, almost arrow straight line 26·4 miles in length. Enginemen were able to better a timing of 19min over this section with their new engines. Both Deal and B Arms men had achieved 80mph plus with the L1s, but the Schools could not only maintain this pace but exceed it; moreover their boilers steamed so well that pressure could be held at 220lb/sq in and their water level maintained. The cut-offs required to reach these speeds were not harsh and the engines rode sweetly. After the hard firing required on an L1 being driven on a full regulator with a cut-off rarely under 30 per cent, the firing of a Schools was decidedly easier. B Arms did not have a Schools of its own until 1935, but worked them on change-over duties.

The remarkable increase in tractive effort then available with these new engines over the inside cylinder types found a place of honour in the Appendix to the Working Time-tables, dated 1934: 'Loads of engines, unassisted between Tonbridge and Tunbridge Wells Central; Class F1 and B1, 190 tons, Class D and E, 220 tons, Class L 250 tons, V (Schools class) 340 tons. This section included a section with a gradient of 1 in 47!

By the middle of 1935, Schools class Nos 900 to 909 were allocated to St Leonards shed (908 went to B Arms in 1947), Nos 910 to 912 to the newly opened Ramsgate shed, and Bricklayers Arms became the settled home for Nos 934 to

13

939. The chargeman cleaner at B Arms at this time saw to it that the new arrivals to the motive power stud were highly polished and enginemen made sure that the footplates sparkled with polished copper and brass fittings.

At the depot there were many characters and, of course, the enginemen's lobby was often the scene of their antics and discussions. Naturally, not all of their incidents occurred in the lobby, but on the footplate, to be recalled before an audience at a later date. Moreover, events at particular locations, on individual engines, or for other reasons could often be remembered for years after by the nicknames applied to the engine or men concerned as a result.

During 1932, the line from Middle Stoke Junction on the Hundred of Hoo Branch, was extended to a point on the Isle of Grain called Allhallows-on-Sea, and the Southern Publicity Department tried to sell this new resort to Londoners. The expected boom never materialised since the shingle and sand beaches of Herne Bay, Margate and Ramsgate were a more attractive location for a day at the sea than the mud-flats of Allhallows.

The large marshalling yard at Hoo was a regular stop for the heavy freight services from B Arms to Queenborough until the end of steam. The wide open spaces of that yard were a scene of constant activity. Gillingham provided the pilot engines for Hoo Yard, busily shunting up and down whilst the train engine from B Arms, Longhedge or Faversham waited patiently for its train to be made-up. A cold winter night at Hoo was a night to remember. Close to Hoo were two stations that gave rise to humorous footplate repartee —Higham and Uralite Halt. A driver would shout to his fireman 'your'a light', 'Who?' 'I'am'!

Close to Hoo were many long abandoned chalk workings —large deepwater lakes which were very dangerous. On the banks grew a pretty pink flower which was actually a weed. Many an unsuspecting fireman has, on his driver's recommendation, picked a bunch of 'flowers' for his girl-friend, keeping them in the tool-bucket, in cold water, until the trip was over. Once the 'flowers' were placed in a warm room they developed an odour that gave rise to their name of 'Cat Weed'; more than one engagement has been broken by their presentation!

In 1934, a modernised locomotive depot was opened at Stewarts Lane, close to the old London, Chatham & Dover depot at Longhedge and adjacent to the London, Brighton & South Coast depot at Battersea. The old LBSC shed was closed and used later as a lorry depot. Stewarts Lane was a mixed depot from the start with South Eastern and Brighton men covering their respective duties, though they were soon integrated as men learned each other's roads. B Arms men still referred to the depot as Longhedge for many years afterwards.

In the same year, another new depot was opened, not far from Bricklayers Arms, at Hither Green, in the Borough of Lewisham. The depot was located on a site, which for many years had been a rubbish dump, in the middle of a triangle formed by the main line to Sevenoaks, the Sidcup route to Dartford (the Dartford Loop Line), and the Lee to Hither Green goods spur. The new depot was immediately dubbed 'The Rubbish Dump' by B Arms men. In later years, this unkind name gave place to a new nickname, that of 'The One Horse Depot'. This referred to the single King Arthur class 4-6-0 stabled there, No 800 *Sir Meleaus de Lile*, which the Old Kent Road men pronounced as 'Melius de Lily'. No 800 was kept in spotless condition and ran Hither Green's only main line passenger train—the 5.42 pm Charing Cross to Dover, which called at Waterloo, London Bridge, fast to Knockholt, then all stations to Dover, the Hither Green men being relieved at Ashford. Many of B Arms N class 2-6-0s were transferred to Hither Green along with some of the freight duties. At the present time Hither Green is still a motive power depot for diesel locomotives.

Hither Green yard, with its vast sidings, played an important part in freight train marshalling, particularly cross-London freights conveying traffic from the Midlands and

North of England to Kent and the Continent. In the 1960s a new Continental freight depot was opened at Hither Green and took over traffic previously handled at Blackfriars and Ewer Street.

After Bricklayers Arms passenger station had closed its doors to normal traffic in 1852, the whole area was given over to freight operation but when the summer passenger programme for 1932 was drawn up, it was decided to reopen Bricklayers Arms station for excursion traffic. An elaborate set of rules to ensure complete safety of passenger trains using the B Arms branch was incorporated in the 1934 Appendix to the Working Timetables. They provided for a pilotman to accompany excursion trains between Rotherhithe Road or Mercer's Crossing and Bricklayers Arms goods shed and for hand or unbolted points to be clipped and padlocked. Trains had to be composed of coaches not more than 8ft wide. These week-end excursion workings ceased in 1939 and were not resumed after the war; excursion trains then started from such inner suburban stations as Deptford or Blackheath.

In 1937, the Southern took delivery of its first three diesel-electric shunting locomotives, numbered 1 to 3. They were built by the English Electric Company and were put to work in Norwood shunting yard. Also introduced in that year were Maunsell's Q class 0–6–0 tender engines mainly for freight; they were useful engines, but many an Eastern Section engineman remarked of them 'they are only a six-wheeled L1', which was very near the truth.

About this time Bulleid, who had succeeded Maunsell, undertook modifications to the exhaust arrangements in an attempt to improve performance of several express passenger classes including the Schools 4–4–0s. Part of the equipment included a large diameter chimney with multiple-jet blast pipe. The first three engines modified were 914 *Eastbourne,* 931 *King's Wimbledon* and 937 *Epsom,* the last mentioned a B Arms engine. New firing techniques were called for and it was said that the big chimney Schools 'chattered at the chimney'. Two years later, in 1939, *Epsom* was given an extended smokebox and a rimless chimney and looked most ungainly until it was again modified with a big chimney, including a rim, in 1940.

Enginemen developed their own style of driving a Schools and most were reluctant to put them in the big valve except when climbing from Tonbridge up to Tunbridge Wells Goods Yard. B Arms men used to refer to the opening of the second valve as 'giving her the lot'. Some drivers would restart a Schools with the cut-off lever in the same position as they ran in—20 or 25 per cent; one B Arms man even used to restart with the lever almost in mid-gear, claiming that she (the engine) would find her own feet.

In April 1939, property speculators had managed to convince the Southern Railway that it would be a good idea to build a station between Swanley and Eynsford to serve a proposed new housing estate and an airport, to be called Lullingstone. The station was completed in April 1939, and stood unwanted and unopened, exactly as it was finished, for 14 years. It was dismantled in the late 1950s, though the platforms and the long station driveway are still clearly visible. It became a regular leg-pull for drivers to ask a new fireman to 'see if there is anybody waiting at the next station'. Like many pre-war plans neither the housing estate nor the airport were ever built, and Lullingstone was always referred to as the ghost station. With the present day hunger for building land maybe Lullingstone estate will be built and then the demolished station that was built too soon will be re-built!

In 1939, the average pay for a driver was, with overtime, around £3 10s 0d a week, and for a fireman about £3 2s 6d. A good fish and chip supper in the Old Kent Road could be had for 6d, and it cost but a penny (an old pre-decimal penny) to ride on the tram from Bricklayers Arms to New Cross Gate. The best seats in the Trocadero Cinema at the Elephant & Castle (complete with Wurlitzer Electric Organ recital of popular tunes, two feature films, a cartoon and the News) would cost a shilling.

B   17

Firemen were in the top link for up to seven years, and had regular engines, which they reckoned to fire at the same spots on the road every time. While helping to sight signals, they learned the name of every signal they passed and the signalbox which controlled it. Firemen would re-pack a leaking gauge glass or replace a broken one on the road, and would not dream of letting a fitter do this for them. Between firing, they polished cab fittings until they shone, and took over the regulator when their driver thought them to be ripe for practical tuition. Most firemen were on the shovel for about 20 years and when they eventually did pass as driver, no men could have been so well-trained or have served such a long apprenticeship as was necessary to become an engine driver in those pre-war days.

The days of long apprenticeships were fast drawing to a close for footplatemen and, indeed, in many other walks of life. The railways of Britain in general and the Southern in particular, because of its geographical location, were about to enter into the second world war. As many older drivers commented 'Here we go again' there were just as many who echoed the popular belief that 'it will all be over by Christmas', though no one was quite sure which Christmas it would be.

2

The second world war and the end of the Southern Railway

The full story of the difficulties and bravery of railwaymen and women have already been fully documented. The war and its subsequent effect on many aspects of railway work and conditions, however, need a background setting for a full appreciation of the immense change from pre-war operation to post-war conditions.

The first demands made on Bricklayers Arms motive power depot, and indeed, many others, came on 1 September 1939 when the mass evacuation of school children from London, and other large industrial towns, was carried out. Overnight, a new word was added to the English language—'evacuee'. Many hospitals sent patients out of London, and to help move this vast mass of children and patients, every engine and engineman available was needed. Bricklayers Arms engines went as far afield as Worcester, Oxford, Eastbourne and many inland towns and villages. The destination of school children was a secret and station platforms were the scene of many heartbreaks for children and parents alike.

The phoney war brought little apparent change to life and very soon, to the relief of their hosts and to the consternation of the authorities, the evacuees began to return home. The expected heavy bombing did not take place and many schools were re-opened in London.

Because of blackout restrictions whether or not an air raid was in progress all engines carried cab-sheets which enveloped the cab during the hours of darkness to shield the glow from the open firehole door, making it too warm in winter and almost unbearable in summer for enginemen.

Every man had to carry a gas-mask and a steel helmet, though firing in a steel helmet was almost an impossibility. To reduce the risk of enemy agents infiltrating the railway system, each man and woman was given an oval brass lapel badge, which bore the words 'Railway Service' in blue. The badge also carried a number which identified the owner. After the war these badges were given to cleaners who wore them until they gained their 'Engineman SR' cap badge when appointed as firemen. Like many everyday railway items the badges are now collectors' pieces.

Situated in the heart of South-East London, close to the docks and London's Tower Bridge, and surrounded by a vast network of railway lines, Bermondsey expected to be hit, and hit hard when the air raids started. With Bricklayers Arms in the middle everyone waited.

The fall of Holland in May 1940 marked the end of the phoney war. Many men, particularly the older ones who had served in France in the first world war, believed that the British Expeditionary Force in France, having stopped the enemy before would do so again. How wrong they were is history now. The fate of some 300,000 men was suddenly at stake when all resistance in France collapsed. The Royal Navy ably assisted by the 'Little Navy' of private sailors carried out the greatest rescue operation in history—Dunkirk.

The nearest British port was Dover, and it fell upon the Southern Railway to get the men away as fast as they were landed. The old road between Tonbridge and Redhill was closed to all ordinary traffic and a traffic control centre was established at Redhill. A minimum of written orders were to be issued. Every available engineman was called upon to help, and even cleaners with little firing experience found themselves suddenly promoted to fireman. Men were instructed to report for duty with a pile of sandwiches, a packet of tea and sugar and a tin of condensed milk and to tell their families that they were running a few extra trains 'down to the coast' and might not be home for a day or two. Every engine that could be put into steam was made ready.

Stirling F1 'Flying Bedsteads', B1s, Ds, 'Germans', L1s, King Arthurs, Schools, D1 and E1 rebuilds, 'Woolworths' (Class N 2–6–0s), the larger-wheeled Class U 2–6–0s and the game old C class 0–6–0s headed down to the coast. Rotherhithe Road, Blackheath and Maze Hill sidings were emptied of every coach. Coming up, trains ran non-stop to Paddock Wood, where the broad platforms laid out for the hop trade, enabled the tired men to be given sandwiches and tea by the women-folk of the village. On to Redhill, where trains reversed for the Reading line, engines were serviced, while fresh loco-motives took their loaded trains on towards destinations as varied as Birmingham and Scotland. Redhill yard at one time was choked with a mountain of engine smokebox ash and clinker. For the engine crews it was a bite to eat and back to the coast. Some crews made three trips up and down. An Army officer asked an engineman what time he would finish duty and got the answer 'Tomorrow, guv'nor'. It was true to say that after two days of 'down and back', many men did not know if they were coming or going. The signalmen worked like slaves and one B Arms driver recalled 'the signals were going up and down like yo-yos', so frequent were the trains. Men were on duty for 48 hours, then went home for a few hours rest and back for another 48.

A few days after it started, it was over. While the Wehr-macht examined the equipment left on the beaches, the ex-owners were already being regrouped and retrained. The vast majority of the British Expeditionary Force was back on British soil. A ticket collector at Dover summed it up when he said '300,000 passengers and not one of them asked me where the train was going!'

As the war dragged on, women joined the railways, as station announcers, ticket collectors, porters and as engine cleaners (not in the line of promotion though) and fitters mates. At B Arms, they worked in the repair shops and helped the shed fitters and began to do little jobs on their own such as gland packing and greasing tender axle-boxes. Some of their efforts were jokingly criticised by enginemen who received hot replies from the lady fitters in language not usually forthcoming from the fair sex. Women made very good guards on passenger trains and engine drivers mockingly complained that the railway had put women behind them to nag them if they lost time. Up to 1947, women guards were on the Eastern Section electric trains out of Cannon Street and Charing Cross. As in nearly all jobs they tackled, the women made excellent substitutes for man-power. There is one station today, on the South Eastern Division that still has a female booking clerk and station staff and golden female voices today announce many trains, even though they are on tape.

After the Battle of Britain and the daytime raids, came the night raids, the railway's 'darkest hours', in more ways than one. For his actions on the night of 14/15 October 1940, Fireman George Russell of B Arms was commended in his coolness and alertness in carrying out duties during heavy bombing between Hastings and Cannon Street when he extinguished fire bombs on the track. The same man was later commended for examining the line between Brockley and New Cross Gate on the night of 16 April 1941. I remember that night as I then lived close to that section of line which suffered hits and near misses from three land-mines, a shower of fire bombs and two aerial torpedoes which removed most of our roof. Fireman Russell walking along the line, to check for possible damage was indeed an example of coolness. George Russell later became an inspector at B Arms and in more recent years went to the Line Managers Office.

The date, 12 November 1940; the place, Angersteins Wharf, Greenwich. A fire bomb raid is in progress and canisters of incendiary bombs are bursting in the sky, showering the sidings with phosphorous. B Arms fireman Jack Glew put out bomb after bomb and prevented much damage that would otherwise have been caused. A few months later, the night of 10/11 May 1941 was one of the worst nights of the blitz and B Arms Driver Len Stainer recorded his experiences that night, thus:

'I booked on duty at 11.05 pm and left the Loco Depot at 11.30 to work the 12.53 am Cannon Street to Dartford (a steam-hauled passenger train). On going up to Cannon Street, between Surrey Canal Junction and London Bridge, a fire had started over by Surrey Docks and loads of incendiaries were dropped all the way to London Bridge and the City. We stopped the engine at Borough Market Junction and my fireman put out the incendiaries. On arriving at Cannon Street, Platform 6, bombs began to drop, then the signal lights went out and some bombs dropped outside the station bringing down clouds of dust.

'A fire had started at the side of the station, and it then rained bombs and there seemed to be no stopping. The fires were then like huge torches and there were thousands of sparks. The smoke from the fires blacked out the moon, and fires seemed to be everywhere, and then, the station roof caught alight.

'To save a train in the station catching fire, two engines coupled together (Schools class 934 and H class 1541) pulled the train out of platform 8 on to the bridge. We had stopped 20yd ahead of the other train, and then after about 10min, we ducked down on the footplate. We counted three bombs, the last one was terrific, and very close. There was a terrific explosion and our engine seemed to roll, at first we thought our train had been hit. The debris flew in all directions—we were very lucky. My fireman said at the time "Look out—we are going in the drink" and I thought my back week had come. We looked round and found that the bomb had made a direct hit on No 934 and it had blasted our train and turned part of the train over on its side. My fireman and myself went to see where the driver and fireman of the Schools were, and I am pleased to say they had just got off the engine in time.'

From the appearance of this article in the *Southern Railway Magazine*, Len Stainer was forever known as 'Old Back Week'. The term back-week referred to the practice of the company to keep one week's pay in hand, and upon death or retirement one was said to have 'drawn your back week'. Poor old Len never forgot that night at Cannon Street, and neither did the driver of the Schools, James Foote, who was awarded the British Empire Medal for his bravery in taking her out on to the bridge. Jim Foote's association with No 934 *St Lawrence* that fiery night was not forgotten by the men at B Arms and for years afterwards 934 was often referred to as 'Footie's engine'.

Foote became a running foreman at B Arms after the end of the war, and was involved in a curious clerical error when the Pay as you Earn income tax scheme was introduced in 1948. For some inexplicable reason, Foote's wife received a letter from the tax department informing her that as she was a widow she was eligible to draw a widow's pension! The men at Bricklayers Arms heard of this and soon afterwards a small coffin was delivered to Jim Foote's home at Petts Wood, bearing the inscription 'His PAYE days are over now!' Jim kept this memento of 'his demise' in his bedroom and a local newspaper commented on the grim humour of his colleagues.

During 1943, Ashford Works produced a new type of o–6–o tender engine, designed by the chief mechanical engineer, O. V. S. Bulleid. This class at first was known as an austerity engine as they did not have running plates and were designed to use the minimum amount of metal in their construction. They looked weird and seemed to have been designed to provoke ridicule, but were most efficient engines. Bulleid adopted the continental system of numbering for his Merchant Navy class Pacifics, introduced in 1941, whereby numbers indicated the leading and trailing axles and a letter the driving axles; the 4–6–2 wheel arrangement of the Merchant Navy was thus described as 21C. Similarly the austerity o–6–os were numbered from C 1 onwards. During the war, the armed services used a phonetic alphabet—A for Apple, B Baker, C Charlie, and so the austerity engines became known as 'Charlies' for ever more. The Southern Railway's official designation of the class, Q1, was rarely used.

The men liked the Charlies, which were powerful engines with a boiler pressed at 230lb/sq in. They moved an immense amount of war traffic and their ability to maintain working pressure with the poor coal then allocated to the railways, put them in favour with their crews. The only bad point about them was the draught in their spartan cabs; a winter's night on a Charlie was no joke for the fireman working for much of his time in front of open fire-hole doors, while the driver, sitting in his corner was subjected to biting draughts that brought forth some equally biting expletives! The engines were equipped with steam reverse gear, not the Stirling pattern from the SECR, which was a dead-beat certainty but the Bulleid design, which tended to 'jump-abaht-a-bit', though not as badly as on the Bulleid Pacifics which at that date had not arrived on the scene. In later years, the Q1s were in regular use on the Hastings goods (via Tunbridge Wells) and the Horsham and Fratton goods (via the Quarry line—the Redhill avoiding line). B Arms used them on the No 123 duty, on which all cleaners had their first (official) trip on the footplate, leaving Sorting Sidings at 10.15 am and running to Tonbridge via Blackheath and Maidstone West, with an unfitted goods train.

At long last, the war ended and with it, the end of an era never to return. The Southern looked forward to a resumption of its boat train traffic, which had been growing steadily before the outbreak of hostilities. Arrears of track maintenance had accumulated, and a general speed limit of 65mph was imposed throughout the whole Southern system. The travelling public, the Southern's main source of income, complained of the slow, so-called express trains, some of which in 1946 were taking longer for their journey times than during the war! Moreover, almost in justification of slow running, the 2.10 pm Victoria to Ramsgate was derailed outside Catford Station on 20 September 1946, part of the train running down the embankment into Catford Greyhound Stadium grounds. Only one man was killed—an RAF pilot—a tragic end to a flying career that had survived the war in the air. At the ensuing enquiry, the Ministry of Transport Inspector, Col E. Woodhouse, said he had heard of the poor riding qualities of the Schools class over that route. The Schools on the 2.10 pm that day was No 917 *Ardingly*, and her driver, S. Marsh, said that he did not consider that the Schools were lively on their springs. The cause of the accident was attributed to a spell of wet weather, which had retarded track maintenance and allowed the track to drop slightly.

While conditions were never to return to pre-war levels, the summer of 1946 was a record for holiday traffic, particularly to the Continent. Many men who had waited patiently on the beaches of Dunkirk in 1940, waited at Victoria, with their families to visit France. In common with many other Southern depots, Bricklayers Arms crews worked long hours to move the queues of holiday makers at Charing Cross, some crews worked down to Hastings and back, then a second trip down and back again! The first general election since the war brought the Labour Party into power with a promise to nationalise many industries, including the railways.

On the morning of Monday, 15 April 1946, Stewarts Lane Duty No Special 1 (later Duty No 4) made its first post-war trip, leaving Victoria precisely at 10 am with Merchant Navy Class 21C1 *Channel Packet* at the head of the all Pullman Golden Arrow. The engine, cleaned to perfection, sported an arrow target on its smokebox door, a Union Jack and a Tricolour flag fluttering from her middle lamp iron and a large wooden arrow pinned to each side of the boiler casing. The immaculate train of chocolate and cream Pullman cars, smelling of fresh paint from their thorough overhaul at Preston Park works, gleamed in the sunlight as the train climbed Grosvenor Bank from Victoria. On the way to Dover Marine, every passing engine gave a long, loud whistle as a salute, and the drivers shouted to their firemen 'There goes the Arrer'. As far as I can discover, Stewarts Lane men always ran 'The Arrer' though B Arms men frequently ran the '2 o'clock' boat train when Stewarts Lane was short of men. The Arrow was the pride of the Eastern Section as was the Bournemouth Belle the prestige train of the Western Section, though this train did not recommence running until six months after the Golden Arrow.

The accident involving *Ardingly* at Catford in September 1946 was hardly forgotten, when on 26 December of the same year, a Weymouth to Waterloo train was derailed at Byfleet; the engine was No 851, *Sir Francis Drake* and track subsidence was to blame. The 65mph limit thus remained.

The opening of 1947 was marked by heavy snowfalls in most parts of England. By the second week in January the weather had deteriorated into what was known as 'the big freeze'. Severe gale force winds kept the colliers in port and then the snow became a blizzard, so severe in the North of England that miners could not get to the pits. Coal already loaded in wagons was marooned in sidings. By 10 February, the Government stopped the supply of coal to industry, resulting in thousands of men and women being out of work. In those days, the Southern generated its own power for its electric trains, but the amount of coal for its power stations was strictly limited. During the day, temperatures rose little above freezing point, while at night ice formed on the conductor rails. Bricklayers Arms supplied 2–6–0s and Schools 4–4–0s to assist electric trains up Forest Hill Bank. Running tender first, the engine crews' overalls froze stiff and snow piled into the corners of the cabs—only a few feet from the fire-hole doors!

In the various shunting yards on the Bricklayers Arms branch, particularly at High Level and Sorting Sidings, enginemen considered themselves fortunate when they watched the shunters constantly falling over in the frozen snow.

The bitter weather continued into February. On one occasion the relief crew waiting at London Bridge for the Dover Mail were amazed to see a foot of snow frozen to the smokebox door of the Schools class engine that brought the train in one morning. Water cranes had fires burning by them for 24hrs a day. Many engines on the Western Section were converted to oil burners in an effort to save coal.

On 4 March, a severe gale with driving rain struck the South of England, the rain turned to snow and the snowstorm developed into a raging blizzard. Delays to steam trains were bad and a Ramsgate crew reported that the sea had frozen at Reculver. Delays to electric trains were far worse—but perhaps the peak of late running was the 4.25 pm fast from Brighton to Victoria, due in at 5.25 pm, which actually arrived at Victoria at 12.40 am just $7\frac{1}{4}$hr late; imagine that written on the lost time ticket. A ticket was normally issued by the guard for time lost in excess of one minute! After the protracted spell of bad weather, the cold spell ended on 10 March with a torrential downpour, which caused numerous earth slips.

By the middle of March the weather had settled down and everyone from the 'Governor', F. L. Howard, to the most junior cleaner at The Brick breathed a sigh of relief. Howard was quite a character; invariably attired in a pin-stripe suit, with a flower in his lapel, he walked round the sheds carrying his rolled umbrella, which remained rolled-up even when it was pouring with rain. It was rumoured that the shed fitters had welded it in the closed position years before and that he had not yet discovered it! He was always polite and precise in his speech and never failed with a 'good morning' or 'good afternoon' to any engineman he passed, when doing his rounds of B Arms. His pet place for inspection was the repair shops (opened in 1934), where wheels were turned and engines stripped down for any urgent repairs. Howard had been a fitter, and his keen interest in what went on in the workshops was more of a practical than managerial nature. The leading fitter at that time was Alf Webster, a small, wizened but genial natured man with white bushy eyebrows. He would wince if he heard an engine go on to the turntable with audible sounds of loose wedges or tight journals. Alf lived at Reading and travelled up each morning on the Great Western express service to Paddington. He loved engines—even Great Western ones—yet many years before at Charing Cross, when a young man, he was seriously

28

burned while attending to a locomotive. He spent a year in hospital and was unable to be shaved. No hair ever grew again on his forearms, yet his eyebrows, which were burned off, grew rapidly, as did a beard, which extended to a great length. The foreman fitter was Bert Wood, who had come from Ashford and immediately after arrival at Bricklayers Arms made his presence felt. The shopping of locomotives was speeded up and serviceability improved. In charge of the shops was Charlie Richford, whose trilby-hatted head could be seen peering into stopped engines and chasing the fitters to 'hurry it up'.

In 1947, the West Country class locomotives appeared on the Eastern Section, though they were really classed as Battle of Britain locomotives, with a special narrow cab to suit the Eastern Section loading gauge. Because of their somewhat tinny casing, the West Country and Battle of Britain class engines were dubbed 'spam cans' or simply as 'spams'. At first the BOB class ran with nameplates covered, until the official naming ceremonies were performed. The coming of the 'spams' brought some electrifying runs, on occasions, and a flow of extra bad language from fitters and enginemen, regularly.

Following the end of the war some 2–8–0 tender engines of the Ministry of Supply design, returned to England after service overseas in France, Germany and Libya. By 1947, the Southern had acquired 25 of them, classed as AY (Austerity), though they were generally referred to as the WD class (War Department). The engines were numbered in the 77000, 78000 and 79000 series of the War Department, quite outside the Southern numbering.

Compared to the N class, the WD was a massive engine. One B Arms driver, George Melville, upon seeing his first WD called it 'the mechanical colossus'—an apt description. They had two 19in by 29in cylinders, coupled wheels 4ft 8½in diameter, boiler pressure 225lb/sq in, with a tractive effort of 34,215lb. The engine weighed 70 tons 5cwt and its tender, which carried 9 tons of coal and 5,000 gallons of water, weighed

$55\frac{1}{2}$ tons. The WD class 2–8–0s were based on the LMS Stanier 8F design ably adapted for war conditions by Mr R. A. Riddles. A total of 1,035 of the WD class were built, 545 by the North British Locomotive Company and 490 by Vulcan Foundry.

So it was that several of the WD class arrived at The Brick early in 1947, one still in its dirty yellow desert camouflage. The WD engines were immediately popular with enginemen on the road. The long narrow firebox demanded careful firing to avoid a lump building up under the brick arch, which then prevented coal being fired to the front of the firebox. If the fireman fired correctly, they steamed freely—whether the load was 40, 60 or 90 wagons! Foreman Gregson was somewhat surprised, therefore, when he received a complaint from Driver Fred Brown and his sweating and tired-out fireman, Peter Moffatt, that a WD would not steam! Driver Brown related how his fireman had worked like a slave from Sittingbourne to Swanley and had failed to maintain pressure. Several enginemen had gathered around and had expressed surprise at the rough trip Fred and his mate had experienced. One of the group was a Driver Bowles who had served with the Royal Engineers, Railway Division, in the Desert in the war, and had worked WD engines with loads far in excess than that on the Ramsgate goods. Fred's mate, Moffatt, had 'fired her continuously and the fire shot out of her chimney like crackers' said Driver Brown, who added that he had her 'notched right up on the D mark!' Roars of laughter greeted this remark, as the D mark was for drifting, the point on the cut-off to be used when steam was shut-off to avoid smokebox ash being drawn into the steam chest by the partial vacuum created in the smokebox when the regulator was shut off. It was little wonder that Moffatt had worked like a slave, since the D mark was equivalent to a cut-off of 60 per cent! From that day on Driver Brown was known as 'Cracker Brown'.

The WD class were distinguishable 'a mile off' by their noisy clanking of their coupling rods and on the footplate they oscillated at 40mph. At 50, the vibration made one appreciate how dice feel shaken in a box, though it kept the shovel-plate full of coal. Their powerful steam brakes were notched to give a finely graduated application to suit all loads. The WD class handled any load and were never equalled by any other Southern class of engine.

But 1947 was to be notable in several ways, not least because it was the last year of the Southern Railway's independent existence. In other ways also it was the beginning of the end of an era because the second world war had changed so much that was familiar or had delayed changes in progress in the 1930s. The area around Bricklayers Arms shed, where many of the enginemen lived, had probably changed little for half a century. Between New Cross and London Bridge were row upon row of terraced cottages dating back, in some cases well back, into the last century. Parts of the Old Kent Road were still cobbled, along which a seemingly never ending stream of trams travelled from 3.30 in the morning to half-past midnight, by which time the all-night No 5 tram route was in service. These trams, which ran every night except Saturday provided the means for many enginemen to get to work, if they lived near to the tram route from Downham Estate. The tram crews were a friendly lot, who invariably left Downham 10min late, but by the time Tower Bridge Road was reached, were on time. Many an engineman has accepted the offer to have a go, clattering through the deserted High Streets of Catford and Lewisham at 35mph, reaching B Arms a bit shaken-up in 15min—a journey that took half an hour in the daytime.

The whole length of the Old Kent Road, was one long line of pubs and cafés, from Graingers Dining Rooms—three-course dinner 1s 9d—to the many fish and chip shops, which continued into the New Cross Road, to the eel and pie shop, next door to The Marquess of Granby public house. The old New Cross Empire was still putting on two shows a day; people queued nightly to get into the cinemas and once a week, New Cross thrilled to the motor cycle roar at the

Speedway Stadium, and another night to dog track racing, rivalling Catford Stadium. All over South London, children made miniature speedway tracks on the many bombed pieces of waste ground, with stripped down pedal bikes; organised teams, wearing their own racing colours raced against each other.

During 1947 the old practice of up main line trains running into Cannon Street and then out to Waterloo and Charing Cross, was revived. The train engine remained coupled at Cannon Street and was thus on the back to Charing Cross while another locomotive acted as train engine. Few people used this service, the revival of which seemed pointless, as it simply added yet another conflicting movement at Metropolitan Junction. The No 9 link firemen from Bricklayers Arms who relieved the main line crews at London were given a taste of running a passenger train from Cannon Street on these trains. After the train was emptied at Charing Cross it ran to Rotherhithe Road, where both engines were uncoupled to run light to B Arms.

The gradual rundown of the former LBSCR New Cross Gate motive power depot not far away from B Arms was under way in 1947; it was opened in June 1839 and was destined to be closed by 1948, though the buildings remained for another ten years.

In anticipation of nationalisation the SR's chief mechanical engineer, O. V. S. Bulleid, retired during the year although his brainchild, the double-ended Leader class locomotive was still taking shape. Bulleid was a steam man and he rejected the idea that steam was dead, or dying on its feet. The advantages of electric and diesel locomotives, which did not require to be turned at the end of each run, spurred him to design a steam locomotive that did not need a turntable, and the Leader class was the result. That it was to be fraught with difficulties and eventually scrapped was no discredit to its designer but rather the measure of the man—Bulleid never took the easy way. By the middle of 1947, the Kentish countryside was invaded by Bulleid's Pacifics and the scene was set for some vigorous running. Bulleid's retirement from the SR was marked by a dinner at the Charing Cross Hotel in June 1947

In December 1947, the appointment of Harry Packham was announced as the new running shed superintendent of Bricklayers Arms depot. F. L. Howard moved up to become assistant divisional motive power superintendent, London East Division, based at Orpington, where the control office was located. Howard continued to visit B Arms attired as usual in immaculate pin-stripe suit, flowered button-hole and still carrying his rolled umbrella.

So ended 1947 and the Southern Railway passed into history after a most eventful 25 years. The massive swing to Labour in the 1945 General Election had forecast the nationalisation of many industries, including the railways and on 1 January 1948, it became a fact. In spite of the general left-wing politics of the railwaymen, they were suspicious of the newly formed British Railways. As many men said at that time 'we knew what to expect if we were on the carpet at Waterloo but what now?' It was very much a case of 'better the devil they knew', but no immediate changes took place at Waterloo. One newspaper published a report by an MP that alleged that railways were 'just a lot of rusting scrap iron'. The enginemen's lobby at The Brick, and other depots no doubt, rang to the many suggestions as to the treatment of this member of parliament, all still now, as then, un-printable!

3

Front shift, back shift

In that last year of the Southern Railway what was it like to start a footplate career? One had to start at the bottom rung of the ladder of promotion, as an engine cleaner. The Southern took lads aged 15 years and over as temporary cleaners, after they had passed a very stiff medical examination at the old South Eastern offices opposite No 1 Platform at London Bridge station. If one considered the medical tough, the eyesight test that followed was even harder. You were seated in a kind of dentist's chair, in a darkened room. In front of you was a small mirror, into which tiny coloured lights were projected in rapid succession—Red, Red, Green, Red, Yellow, Purple and Red appeared as a constant pin-cushion of lights. When the examiner was satisfied that the candidate was not colour blind (and a high proportion of young lads were rejected because of this defect), one emerged into a brightly lit room to look at a book which at first glance seemed to consist of nothing but coloured bubbles and dots. As the pages were flicked over, numbers could be discerned amidst the mass of bubbles, which had to be shouted out as quickly as possible. The doctor then handed the candidate a small piece of paper to be returned to the motive power depot which you had applied to join.

At Bricklayers Arms, the paper was given to the chief clerk, Dudley Miles, who instructed the newcomer to report at 8 o'clock Monday morning, to Tommy Tupper, the chargeman cleaner. It was a bitterly cold Monday, in January 1947, that I and several other lads, reported at The Brick. As in every railway depot, safety was always top priority. It was the custom for new cleaners to start at 8 am on their first

34

day (7 am—3 pm for the rest of the week) draw their overalls and rule books from the stores and then accompany the chargehand cleaner to the passageway connecting the running foreman's office to the case containing shed rules, next to which the engineman's notices and alteration sheets were posted. Each cleaner had to read aloud the rules of the shed which included 'No one shall, under any circumstances, pass between engines less than 6ft apart'. It was standard enginemen's practice to park engines buffer to buffer unless the engine required to be moved for fitters running repairs, in which case the engine would then be parked 'six feet off' from the next engine. One Monday morning, the shed enginemen were moving some dead engines in the old shed. The fireman was walking back to couple-up another dead engine and waving his driver back on to this engine; when the line of engines were one length off, the fireman signalled his driver to stop, which he did. The driver sounded the whistle and at a snail's pace proceeded to back-up to the last dead engine, suddenly when only 2ft separated the engines a figure ran between them and even as the engines stopped, he was trapped between them. He was a new cleaner who, only ten minutes before, had read aloud the cardinal shed rule. He died almost instantly with a cry I will never forget—his life in railway service, just twenty minutes. Shed rules were not made to be broken.

My first duty was to clean a class N 2–6–0, No 1823. As the youngest hand, by age, I was allocated the tender. The senior cleaner loudly proclaimed to the new hands not to bother to clean above the level of the engine's cab lights, since the chargehand cleaner could not see above that level from the ground! When no locomotive was available for cleaning, the cleaners were put to good use clearing smokebox ash and clinker. Under 16 year olds worked two shifts—front shift from 7 am to 3 pm, and back shift, 2 pm to 10 pm; over 16 year old cleaners worked a night shift from 10 pm to 6 am. The youngest cleaner was given the covetted job as loco messenger, in which he travelled to various motive power depots, collecting urgently required locomotive spares, delivered mail to the divisional offices, and 'fetched and carried' for various people from the chief clerk to the head of stores. To enable the messenger to travel freely about the Southern, he was loaned a mauve cab pass, for which he signed. He was, however, told not to attempt to ride in the cab of an engine or electric train, since he might distract the driver from his duties. On the back shift turn, the messenger had to travel to Orpington each evening to collect special engine workings, which were duplicated there. Since several B Arms men were 'on the juice' (electrics), it did not take long to learn which drivers, upon seeing the messenger waiting at Waterloo (Eastern) station, would toot the whistle and invite the lad to ride up front with him! The back shift messenger then informed his opposite number on front shift the name of the driver.

Engine cleaners up to the age of 16 were paid 40s 6d for a 48 hour week. Their last six weeks as cleaners were packed with practical work on engines, to prepare them for firing duties. Five weeks were spent with the shed fitters and in which time one learned much about big ends, coupling and connecting rods, injectors, glands, ports, admiralty ferrules, piston rings and many other parts. For my part, my helping hand to the fitters consisted of handing them various spanners, tommy bars and the fitters master tool—the hammer. I learned much from Jim Leggatt and his mate Charlie Bennett; their vocabulary was as varied as the many parts of an engine and the more inaccessible the part, the stronger the expletive. As Leggatt said, when my five weeks with him were completed, 'You know more about engines than you did but I doubt if you could have attended a better school for swearing than B Arms!' Finally there came a running trip, on No 123 duty, on the 10.15 am goods from Sorting Sidings to Paddock Wood via Blackheath and Maidstone, with Driver Bill Parsons and Passed Fireman Cyril Young. The engine was one of Bulleid's Q1 Charlies and a good time was had by all, even if Bill had several shovelfuls of coal dropped on his feet by 'the third man'. On my sixteenth birthday, my name appeared on the alteration sheet as 'fireman' on a shunting engine, signing on at 11 pm and finishing at 8.30 the next morning. The engine was No 2463, an LBSC class E4 0–6–2T, and her driver informed me at the end of the shift that I could not fire to my mother's kitchen boiler! First year firemen earned a basic wage of £4 18s for 48 hours. With the shortage of firemen, resulting in much overtime, my first week's firing pay was £9 15s.

Enginemen worked a 13 day fortnight, having, in theory, every other Sunday off. Like as not, it would often work out that you finished Saturday night's work around 11 am Sunday morning and had to leave home at 11 pm Sunday night in order to start the earliest front shift duty at 12.05 am Monday morning! Often the average working week consisted of not less than 60 hours. Such was life in 1947. It is interesting to note that first year firemen way back in 1870 were earning 21s for a 72 hour week.

With the gradual run-down of New Cross Gate depot, most New Cross duties were still carried out by its own drivers but as these duties were shunting or, at the most, taking empty coaches to London Bridge, the junior duties were given to the most junior B Arms firemen since the New Cross men had been transferred away.

Working at 'The Gate', the B Arms men found they were in a different world. The old 'Brighton' atmosphere clung heavily, with its few remaining men carrying on in their own, fast fading way of life. The new arrivals could be told to 'see to No 75 on two road in the Croydon shed'. The B Arms fireman, after walking around would eventually find a class I3, numbered 2075, in a roofless shed, and would realise that the New Cross men still referred to their engines by their old pre-grouping numbers. The 'Croydon' shed sheltered its last London & Croydon Railway engine back in 1846, but that was 101 years before!

New Cross was a fascinating place. Its octagon layout made it a close, yet spacious depot. During 1947, many types of old LBSCR engines visited it. There were the really beautiful J class 4–6–2 tank engines from Tunbridge Wells, which could just manage to be turned on the small turntable at New Cross, the gallant I3 class, which often found the climb up to Oxted, with nine on, a bit much, but how they roared through New Cross Gate from London Bridge with the evening trains. By Honor Oak Park, the I3 driver would, in all probability, have advanced the cut-off to 40 per cent in order to pass Forest Hill in 9min while his mate was firing expertly through the tip-flap firehole door that B Arms men found so difficult to master. The pride of the enginemen at New Cross was hard for them to conceal when the Atlantics, after servicing in New Cross, later thundered through with the businessmen's 4.20 pm from London Bridge. New Cross men, when you got to know them and could prove to them that you could fire their engines, would often relate how, as a fireman, they had worked the Atlantics on the Brighton fasts, in days gone by.

Others would recall the terrible I1 class, and how on a fast train, one would pass Star Lane box (between Coulsdon and Merstham tunnel on the Quarry Line avoiding Redhill) with 80lb of steam and an inch of water showing in the gauge glass, yet they still kept going! The turntable at New Cross was not big enough to turn an Atlantic, so that they had to make a triangular turn via the Old Kent Road Spur (now dismantled), rounding the sharp curves close by New Cross Stadium and Millwall Football Club, where the sleepers would groan as the Atlantic made its stately way round.

At night, one sole engineman and a fireman were the only staff at the old New Cross Loco. The fireman would tour the yard at two hourly intervals to check on the fires and the water levels of the half-dozen engines left over-night. The last governor at New Cross, George High, came in at 8.00 each morning to deal with paper work, though by the middle of 1947, all time-sheets were sent daily to B Arms time office by the messenger. On the walls of George High's office were photogravure prints of old Brighton engines such as *Charles*

C. Macrae, Gladstones and Grey Ladies, and copies of engine workings going back well before the outbreak of world war two were stacked neatly in the large cupboards along the wall facing the windows. The few drivers remaining—and soon to be transferred to B Arms—still signed on in the time office just inside the gateway leading from Brighton Grove. The gateway and entrance is still standing today and is used by the Carriage & Wagon Department, as is one of the old buildings. The old Brighton atmosphere still hangs around there, though the engine sheds have long since been demolished and 12 car electric trains now berth where engines used to stand.

After two weeks of New Cross, the fireman would be paired with a driver and get on the roster in the lowest link—the 'as required' gang. The title is self explanatory and had some very varied signing-on times which would be advised by the daily alteration sheet. For example, in the first week, the front shift might run: Sunday, 4 am; Monday, 2 am; Tuesday, 12.05 am; Wednesday, 2 am; Thursday, 4 am; Friday, 4 am; and Saturday, 6 am. Such a varied range of times soon sorted out those who could get up early and those who could not. The jobs allocated on these duties were preparation and disposal of engines, and 'seeing away'. This involved making up the fire, shovelling forward to the front of the tender coal that would be needed on the trip, topping up the tender water supply, and putting in all oil trimmings and setting the lubricators, so that all the relieving men had to do was drive off.

Very often, after being on duty for two or three hours, the fireman would be drafted to a running turn in place of the regular fireman who had not shown up for duty. After a few weeks in the as required gang, most firemen had been down the main line at least once and though they might have had a rough trip they were all the more useful firemen proving the truth of the saying 'there is no substitute for experience'. Most enginemen used to say that there is always something to learn on every trip and since each engine was

39

an individual—even those of the same class—every trip taught the fireman something.

Most as required duties were allocated by the running foreman literally as and when he required them, so that when several spare firemen were available (a rare event) he would use his judgment in selecting a man to fire to an upper link driver. The running foremen at B Arms were, at this period, some of the best it ever had.

For many years, the list clerk, at B Arms, was George Hart (Hartie) whose unenviable job it was to compile the daily alteration sheet which of course affected all crews at different times. George knew all the men's seniority by heart, and allocated extra duties in strict order of seniority. This entailed taking men off their rostered duties, thereby causing some inconvenience. Men could be moved two hours either way from their rostered time, that is a man rostered for 3 am could be moved to 1 am or 5 am. It was the rule that all men should return to B Arms to look at this sheet after they had completed a day's work, but it became the unwritten rule that crews relieving should write down the driver and fireman's altered duty number and time of signing on. If alterations had to be made after the crew had finished duty, and they lived within five miles of the depot, a cleaner would be despatched to their home, with a buff coloured call note. It was often pushed through the letter box, in the early hours, after the letter box had been well and truly rattled!

Let us go into the passageway outside the foreman's office. Enginemen are signing on and studying the notices, others queue for the extra tea, sugar and milk rations being handed out by one of the union men, for Britain was still rationed in the late 1940s, and enginemen qualified for extra rations. Soap was also being issued—one tablet a month. The usual remarks are being made to the issuer that it looked more like a piece of cheese than soap and that one would get a better wash from cheese. Even so, the issued soap used to lather if a little soda was added. Anti-dermatitis cream was also issued. The running foreman on duty, Fred Pankhurst

(Panky), emerges from his small smoky office. On his head is jammed a greasy trilby hat, his waistcoat is covered in cigarette ash, and there is a cigarette end in his mouth. He stalks up to the lobby at the far end of the corridor and stands at the doorway where the as required men are, as usual, talking shop. A young fireman holds court, relating his experience the previous week on the Hastings newspaper train: '. . . I had that Schools right round on 220 all the way from London Bridge as far as . . .' Panky interjects 'Peak Freans'. A roar of laughter greets this timely interruption as one way to take a boasting fireman down a peg was to say that he had done well for steam all the way from London Bridge to Peak Freans (one mile!). 'Now', said Panky, 'go and relieve that fireman on that Brighton tankie out there and for Gawd's sake hurry up or the fire will be out'. The fireman's driver gets up and asks Panky how his mate got on when he stood-in on the Hastings paper train. Panky smiles and says 'Well—I have not seen a ticket (lost time) so he must have done all right—but don't tell him I said so'.

The supply of as required men is quickly exhausted and crews arrive on the coal-stage after 10 or 11 hours on duty and ask for relief. Panky pleads, flatters and finally manages to get them not only to put the engine away but get it ready as well, just to 'help him out'. The phone rings and the telephone clerk informs Panky that the fireman due to sign on at 5.15 pm is ill, so that the 6.18 pm from Cannon Street is without a No 2 link fireman—and the 6.18 is often a target for the evening press. . . . Panky answers that the fireman already up at Cannon Street only signed on at 2.30 pm so that a breath of Kentish air won't do him any harm. Panky returns to his office and soon a blue haze of acrid smoke fills the corridor. A driver loudly remarks that someone must have lit-up a 'Spam' but his fireman blithely replies that the smoke is from one of Panky's cigarettes made from his own special recipe of shredded cleaning rags!

A little later on, Panky sees out of the corner of his eye, a driver and his fireman signing on. Due to the heavy evening traffic in Old Kent Road the crew are late and are due away from Cannon Street in under 40min. They turn to read the notices but Panky's voice booms out all they want to know 'No water at Tonbridge, down side, temporary speed restriction of 40 miles an hour this side of Marden station—when you come back tonight run two minutes later from Tonbridge—off you go'. The crew thank Panky and his photographic memory and set off for Cannon Street.

Enter a fireman off an engine taking coal. 'I've been on for 10 hours and have not eaten for six. . . .' Panky looks up and enquires 'What—are you dieting?' 'No' comes the reply 'I've been on for . . .' 'All right, all right son—just you go up to the canteen and have a nice bacon sandwich after you've put her away and then you will be able to get her ready for 81 duty'. The fireman leaves the little office and 'helps him out'. Pankhurst was a first class foreman. He knew how to get the best out of men, even when they had already done more than a day's work. Fred Pankhurst could read through a set of engine workings and then recite them. No man ever saw him refer to working sheets and few men disputed his knowledge of them. Those who did, were invariably proved wrong.

Another pair of top link men sign on, the driver, a gruff-voiced man with a scarf wound around his neck in the style known as a 'choker', puts his head inside Panky's office. 'What one have you got for us tonight?' he enquires. Without consulting any notes the reply comes back '21C 177'. 'A b . . . . . Spam, again' says Bill Parsons to his fireman, Cyril Young. Pankhurst looks back at Bill and says: 'Always moaning, ain't he Cyril—I bet he was a miserable stoker when he fired to old George Stephenson on the flaming *Rocket!*' Cyril cuts in 'Now be fair, Panky, Bill's not that old—he never fired to George Stephenson on the *Rocket* but his son, Robert!' The quick-fire repartee brought several chuckles from other men and as Bill and his mate walked up to Swan Gate to catch a No 46 Tram to Cannon Street, Bill was still mumbling that he had never even driven the *Rocket*, let alone fired her!

Into Panky's office bursts Driver Syd Nibbs—never been known to have his shirt done up, even in the depth of winter. 'So help me, Fred, I told that . . . . . 'erbert you gave me to put her away. Guess what—he's . . . . been and gawn and done? He's chucked all the . . . . . fire out of her, the . . . . . idiot'. 'All right, Nibbo,' replies Pankhurst, 'keep your hair on—there's a Schools next to you on two road, isn't there— so get that stoker of yours to take some of her fire and relight your engine so as to be ready for 581 duty'. Driver Nibbs left the foreman's office mumbling that well-worn phrase to the effect that 'You don't get firemen nowadays—they all died, years ago!'

Fred Pankhurst left B Arms early in 1951 to become running foreman at Stewarts Lane. When he arrived there, a few of the enginemen thought they could pull the wool over 'that bloke from B Arms' by baffling him with the Stewarts Lane duties. Fred, however, had read through the whole of the duty rosters before taking up his appointment, and argued with the men concerned, until they had to admit that they were just 'trying one on'. Fred's trilby, ash covered waistcoat and gruff voice—with a heart of gold beneath— soon won respect. In 1952, a real 'foreign' (ie not Southern) governor took charge of Stewarts Lane, R. N. Hardy, off the Eastern Region. Fred proved to be of great help to the new governor, without losing the respect of his men by the simple rule of remembering that Stewarts Lane men were Southern men, and what one region did, it did not follow that it would be tolerated by Southern men.

Whenever a B Arms crew went into Stewarts Lane, Fred's voice would boom out their names (and cast doubt on their parentage) and receive back a suitable reply couched in terms only the men of Old Kent Road could warmly appreciate. Beneath the torrent of abuse that would be exchanged from the foreman's office and the footplate of the visiting engine-men, lay the very basis of understanding that Panky knew and loved. I was very sorry to learn of the death of Fred Pankhurst, while preparing this book. but such was his stature, many men who had worked with him attended his funeral.

The next foreman to come on duty is Fred Gregson, always referred to as 'Sos'. No one could explain why Fred Gregson gained this nickname—which was the abbreviation used on a lost time ticket to denote 'short of steam', since his exploits on the shovel were legendary. Many years earlier, when in the top link at B Arms, Fred, after cleaning the fire, emptying the ash-pan and the smokebox of his regular L1 upon arrival at Dover, then oiled her up. His driver had adjourned to a nearby refreshment house. Like all firemen in those far-off days, Fred had been years on the shovel and had already completed about six years in No 1 link. When his driver arrived on the footplate, about five minutes before starting time, Fred, outspoken as ever, commented on the fact that he did not consider that his driver was in a fit state to take the train (fast from Folkestone Central to Waterloo (Eastern) in 77min) to London. His driver replied 'If that's how you feel about it you can be driver and fireman' and left the footplate, to ride in the train.

Fred brought the train up to Charing Cross doing the job of driver and fireman. When asked about this incident many years later, the reply I received was 'Yes—I remember that trip up—first lost time ticket my mate had with me—for two minutes!' Bearing in mind that the L1 was not an easy engine to fire, Fred observed all signals without difficulty; he remarked 'We were firing for so long in the 1920s and 1930s, we knew where we were blind-folded, the name of every signalbox and signals it controlled. One counted the rail joints when firing—you knew just where to look out for the signals that way'. Even so, it was a superb, though irregular, demonstration of enginemanship.

Approaching London you learned to know just where you were by the smells. Once past New Cross one would smell the sweet odour of confectionery from the factory of W. S. Shuttleworth, at Blue Anchor Lane (now demolished). On your right the mouth-watering smell of baking biscuits indicated Peak Freans, at Spa Road. A little further on, the left-hand side soon reeked of the vinegar brewery of Messrs Champions (now Sarsons)—by this time, if the train was booked to stop at London Bridge, speed should have been down to 30mph.

Sos Gregson had a habit of cadging tobacco off any willing or unsuspecting engineman—particularly from any young fireman who had just taken up smoking. One night, Driver Joe Bond decided to teach Sos a lesson and instructed me to get Sos to come and have a look at the rotten selection of coal our WD 2–8–0 had been supplied with. Sos left his pipe on his desk and walked over to our engine to have a look. Joe seized hold of Gregson's pipe and filled it with a drop of superheated oil (thick as treacle when cold), a pinch of coal-block dust, topped by a thin layer of twist tobacco. Many enginemen were aware of the joke and suddenly found it necessary to re-read the special notices, posted in the passageway leading to Gregson's office. Sos returned with me, having convinced me that the WD would steam perfectly on the coal supplied. He picked up his pipe and thanked Joe Bond for filling it for him. This was the moment that everyone was waiting for and if Fred Gregson detected the air of expectancy, he gave no sign of it. A thin blue haze of smoke wisked upwards from the foreman's pipe as the burning tobacco touched the thin layer of coal dust, Gregson, however, smoked on. Men came into his office to get their stabling instructions for their engines, whether they should be put away, got ready, or whether the engine should be engine or tender first into the shed. Generally engines were put engine first into the shed, but several duties for the Schools involved taking empty trains into Cannon Street and then out again to Charing Cross, so that these locomotives had to go out tender first. Gregson finished the almost lethal pipeful without a suspicion of a cough. Joe Bond turned to me, and amidst roars of laughter from the crowd of onlookers, shook his head and said 'He ain't human'. Gregson's final comment, however, brought the house down; he turned to the enginemen standing around and remarked 'Have you not seen a driver give a foreman a pipeful of his best baccy before?'

A few nights after the tobacco incident, Fred Gregson's imperturbability was demonstrated yet again. Around 12.30 am a WD 2–8–0 was due to run light to Sorting Sidings and Fred noticed that, amongst all the noises that make up a locomotive depot, he had not heard the unmistakable sound of that WD clanking out of the yard. He walked over to No 5 road Old Shed and found that a fitter was vainly trying to tighten a gland in the cab that was blowing steam badly on the fireman's side of the footplate. The fitter had three sponge cloths wrapped around his hands to protect them from the steam, but try as he did, he could not tighten the offending gland nut. Gregson looked up at the driver; 'You stay here much longer Bondie, you'll have grass growing out of the bissel'. Joe Bond looked down from his lofty perch and jerked his thumb in the direction of the sweating fitter 'Waiting for 'im'. Gregson climbed aboard and took the spanner from the fitter's hands and without any protection to his hands put the spanner into the blowing steam and with one turn tightened the offending nut and as he left the footplate said to the amazed fitter 'If you don't get off this contraption you are all set for a ride to Queenborough'. Once again Joe remarked to me 'He ain't human'. As we pulled away from the shed, Gregson shouted out 'Neither are you Joe, to smoke your tobacco!'

The chief stores clerk at B Arms was Ernest Baughen. In his younger days he had been a cleaner at The Brick, but had been run over by an engine which had cost him one of his legs. Nevertheless, he was a robust, cheerful character who had the responsibility of ordering every item required in the depot. Ern was on good terms with stores clerks at depots as far apart as Ramsgate and Bournemouth. Liaison was carried out, in those days, by the staff of room 133, at Waterloo station general offices. Very often the B Arms messenger would climb up on to the footplate of a Lord Nelson 4–6–0 at Waterloo (Western), to collect a much needed part that had been put on the tender by another loco messenger from Eastleigh. Ern's vocabulary was often stretched to its most descriptive when an urgently needed part did not arrive, for then Charlie Richford, the B Arms works foreman, would be banging his fist on Ern's table. All firemen used to meet Ernest Baughen at least once in their career, when they had completed the requisite number of firing turns to qualify for their 'Engineman SR' cap badge.

The stores issued oil, paraffin, and head board discs (always referred to as 'boards'), and that item rarely seen out of a driver's hands—the wiper, or to give it its proper name, the sponge cloth. Each engineman was issued daily with a new sponge cloth, which was white, with green thread running through the centre. This gave rise to its nickname of 'a green liner'. Each man was also issued with a washed sponge cloth, known as 'a brown 'un', which was really a 'greenliner' that had been washed at Ashford laundry. The brown wipers were used to wipe cab-lights, clean gauge and head lamps and generally to clean-up. The green-liners were used just to keep hands clean, and were issued on a strictly one for one basis.

In these days of social security it is hard to realise that less than 30 years ago sick pay was in its infancy. 'No work—no pay' was the rule, even if men were off ill. Every pay day, one was reminded of that fact by the collections held for men who had been off sick for some time and were finding it hard to live with no wages coming in. A union man would set up a table close to the pay window. On this table would be an upturned engineman's greasetop cap and a small card naming the man, his wife and children. Every man would put something in the hat—except one engineman who stoutly maintained that men should save for emergencies and not rely on charity. The money collected was taken that night and often exceeded the man's expectations and was always greatly appreciated. Some years later, the man who scorned giving was himself off sick for many weeks and finally appealed for help. His cap remained empty.

4

British Railways and the Bulleid Pacifics

The first months of the newly-formed British Railways administration saw little direct change as far as enginemen were concerned, at least in shed procedure and management. There were of course the visible changes in livery as the new BR numbering system was gradually applied in which ex-Southern engines had their numbers increased by the addition of 30,000 so that class V Schools 4-4-0 No 934 (Footie's engine), for example, became 30934. In due course as well came colour changes. From the operating viewpoint more important was the arrival on the Eastern Section of more Bulleid Pacifics, both the Merchant Navy and the lighter West Country/Battle of Britain classes. The naming of the West Country and Battle of Britain classes seemed haphazard at first but by 1950 the following pattern emerged; 34001–34048 West Country of which Brighton had 34036–34041, 34049–34090 were Battle of Britain, 34091–34108 West Country, and finally 34109 and 34110 were Battle of Britain. By 1950 no West Country or BOB engines were shedded at B Arms, but Stewarts Lane had 34033–34035, 34066–34071 and 34076, 34083–34085, 34091, 34092 and 34101–34104. Ramsgate had Nos 34077–34082, 34086–34090 and 34096–34100 and Dover was allocated 34072–34075. Of course, from time to time engines were changed around, but this was the general location of these engines in the early 1950s.

As more spams came into service, more needed repairs. The fitters hated them from the start and their language took on a new turn of expletives. At that time no spams were shedded at B Arms, but Dover and Ramsgate engines which

Although Bricklayers Arms shed for most of its life served the Kent Coast lines, from 1948 it took over New Cross Gate shed duties which widened the territory of its engines and men to include former LBSCR lines in Sussex, including Oxted. Here the crew of a 'Midland', one of the LMS Fairburn 2-6-4Ts built at Brighton, take water at Oxted, in 1952.

C. R. L. Coles

Bricklayers Arms depot during the period of this book: *above*, SECR Class E 4-4-0 No A175 stands outside the Old Shed in the late 1920s. *Below*, almost at the end of steam Class C 0-6-0 No 31293 simmers outside Old Shed, with its rebuilt roof following war damage, in March 1961.

Locomotive & General Railway Photographs; D. T. Cobbe

came into The Brick for servicing provided the fitters with more than their share of spam teething troubles, troubles which dogged them for the rest of their working lives in the condition as built. The oil bath was a constant source of complaint, leaking oil on to the track, causing much of the slipping that came to be known amongst enginemen as a 'spam start'. Moreover, the oil caused fires under the lagging and in the ash-hoppers. A Stewarts Lane crew had a nasty experience with a boat train from Victoria, when the engine caught fire and the fire brigade was called to them at Bromley South; power to the third rail was cut off and chaos reigned for some time outside and inside the Bromley area.

If the oil-bath was all right then it was almost certain that the valve-chain was in need of adjustment. This clever, but unreliable invention of Bulleid, which did away with the conventional valve gear and associated rods, was probably the 'Achilles heel' of the Bulleid Pacifics. The valve chain links stretched soon after adjustment and affected the valve timing and setting. The steam-operated reverser (itself a curse as it flew forwards and backwards at a mere touch) was also affected so that the estimation of cut-off was strictly by ear. When one reads of finely and honestly documented footplate runs on a spam describing 18 or 24 per cent cut-offs with $\frac{3}{8}$ regulator, I am sure that many an ex spam handler has a little chuckle. I do not doubt that the learned observer did note, most carefully, the cut-off in use, but with the Bulleid gear it was often a case of give or take 20 per cent of the reading. While an experienced driver could drive by ear and feel his engine's response to variations in cut-off, had these powerful locomotives been fitted with conventional valve gear and simple screw reverse, many of their problems would never have arisen. As it was, even the style of driving was dictated by the behaviour of the steam-reverser. The usual method was to find a spot at which the pointer would stay and then drive on the regulator. Many drivers sat all the way with one hand holding down the steam reverse lever to try to stop the cut-off from wandering. Other drivers used to chalk-mark the chosen point and the tip of the indicating pointer so that they could observe movements of the cut-off. Enginemen used to comment adversely on the gadgetry of these engines and paraphrase a well-known saying: 'I think these modern engines are wonderful'. It was hard for fitters and footplatemen to understand how, after 120 years of locomotive experience, these engines came out full of snags. The spams' appetite for coal at times was voracious, and many firemen called them the miner's friend. The idea of designing an engine without the benefit of dampers has never been fully explained even now. In spite of their faults and the amount of money that had to be paid in compensation for the number of lineside fires they caused, the management must have been pleased with them and expanded the original order from 70 to 110.

The position of the sand boxes on the Pacifics made it necessary for special movable platforms to be provided at depots to give access for filling. The boxes were fitted with sliding doors, which sometimes became jammed in the shut position; on a quick turn-round there was no time for a fitter to get up to Ewer Street and a spam with an empty sand box was a tricky engine to handle, particularly through Polhill or Sevenoaks tunnels which were always dripping wet.

When the West Country class first came to Bricklayers Arms, the preparation and disposal firemen complained about the high cab temperatures when cleaning the fires. Several ex-Army drivers who had then only recently returned to England from the Libyan desert, scorned the firemen and said that only in the desert was it really hot. Some firemen then used to hold a contest to see which one could clean a West Country fire in the shortest time, without removing overall jacket, cap or serge jacket! The respective drivers would ensure that the fire was properly cleaned. After the contests, the thirsty stokers would adjourn for 20min to 'The Swan', 'Magnet' or 'World Turned Upside Down' to the delight of the landlord, where the winner was treated to several pints by the losers, who also drank their fill!

We must not though forget the credit-side of these engines. Their ability to get-away with a train, climb gradients as if they had been levelled and be able to steam with the worst coal supplied, are not easily forgotten. When they were in fine-fettle, nothing could touch them. Their exploits in the 1948 locomotive exchanges have been well documented and need no repetition here. To appreciate their finer points when compared to other engines, only a trip on their foot-plate, could do this. They could haul any train that could be put behind them but it was their serviceability that marked them as 'the engines that nothing can beat when they are all right—but they are not all right most of the time'. In later years many were rebuilt with conventional Walschaerts valve gear and the Bulleid novelties disappeared. The rebuilds thus had all the good points of the originals but lost most of the bad details and were superb machines as a result. But that is another story.

To visiting enginemen, the layout of Bricklayers Arms Motive Power Depot was a puzzle. At Ramsgate or Stewarts Lane, one got coal, turned and went into the shed more or less in a straight line. At B Arms after coaling an engine could turn and go on to 8, 7, 5 or 4 road, Old Shed, but if the engine was to be stabled on 6, 3, 2 or 1 road, Old Shed, then it had to come back down the turntable road, through the slip-road, out to Dunton Road bridge and back into the Old Shed, as these tracks did not have a through connection from the turntable. The engine also had to come back down the turntable road if the engine was to be stabled in the carriage shed. All this was a little confusing to visiting enginemen, and wherever possible, they were relieved on the coal road. However, at busy times, when no relief crews were available, the duty running foreman made a point of mentioning that the turntable road was reversible. To complicate matters still further, the turntable was out of sight until the end of the stores buildings was passed (see diagram on page 7) so that even B Arms men tended to move very cautiously when approaching the turntable. The turntable, incidentally, was known irreverently as 'the rupture machine' since it was turned by muscle power only, and with a Pacific or Arthur to turn it was a trial of strength.

A peculiar, and dangerous, aspect of the layout was No 1 road on the Carriage (or St Patrick's) Shed which had an inspection pit which extended to within 2yd of the turntable road and allowed two engines to be over the pit and outside the shed. The leading engine was then foul of the turntable road and it was the duty of the fireman to stop engines on the turntable road until the engine was set back into the shed. B Arms men had lived with this dangerous arrangement since re-modelling of the depot was carried out in the 1870s, but an accident had to happen at this spot one day.

One morning, in 1948, B Arms driver Hooker had to oil up an ex-Brighton tank, No 2113, an E1 0–6–0T. He moved the engine into the open on No 1 road, Carriage Shed, and stopped his engine set right for oiling. His fireman was only newly appointed and without checking the position of the engine, went to the stores for oil. Driver Hooker went underneath to oil-up and must have assumed that his fireman was keeping watch on the turntable road or failed to notice that he was foul of it.

On the coal-stage a Ramsgate Arthur and its crew waited in vain for relief, so the foreman asked the visiting enginemen to put her on 7 road Old Shed and screw her down (ie put the hand-brake hard on and leave her). The foreman warned the Ramsgate men to keep a sharp look out as the shed pilot was moving engines and the turntable might not be in position. It was general practice to return the table to the turntable road after use. The Arthur moved off, with the fireman leaning out on his side of the cab (the right) to get the earliest possible view of the table. The driver crossed the footplate after checking his side, but the boiler of the Arthur obscured No 1 road of the Carriage Shed, and he did not see Driver Hooker's engine standing there. The Arthur struck the little tank engine, pushing it backwards and in so doing crushed Driver Hooker who was, at that moment, still in the motion, oiling up. He was killed instantly. The result of this tragic accident was the filling-in of the pit on No 1 road.

Most major steam depots had a breakdown crane and Bricklayers Arms was no exception. It consisted of two grey-painted ex-SECR birdcage coaches lettered in white, 'Locomotive Running Department', and a 36 ton Ransomes & Rapier steam crane, DS 1197. The breakdown train was always stabled on the road adjacent to the Carriage Shed with the crane in steam at all times. Around the mess coach was a perpetual aroma of pickled onions, since cream-crackers, cheese and a huge jar of pickled onions formed the menu for breakdown crews. The crews were drawn from the fitting staff by day, and from the shed fitters at night plus key men who were on call. The night shed-fitters had a small lobby where their spare moments were spent. Their breakdown clothes—old overalls, enginemen's serge jackets etc—were hung on the wooden wall of the lobby. Every night, around 1 am the fitters would walk up the Hay Road to the canteen for their breakfast of tea, bacon sandwiches and that rare B Arms delicacy—hot buttered rock-cakes. Once or twice a year, the night cleaning gangs would enter the fitters' lobby, in their absence, and tack their breakdown clothes to the wall; as the fitters walked back from the canteen the cry would go up 'Pitch-in at . . .' The fitters would rush into the lobby and grab their clothes from the pegs leaving behind jacket sleeves and trouser legs pinned neatly to the wall. Blood curdling threats would ring through the Old Shed while the cleaning gangs worked steadily on, impervious to the annoyed fitters! These rare incidents were not encouraged as practical jokes in a locomotive depot, often murky from newly lit-up locomotive fires and the constant greasy nature of the walk-ways, could end in a fatality. Sky-larking was strictly forbidden and rightly so; humorous and harmless leg-pulling, however, was reserved for new hands. The stores received a steady demand from new firemen and cleaners for such items as red tail-lamp oil, left-handed firing shovels, whitewash for inside the smokebox door, furniture polish for the driver's chair and other unlikely locomotive stores.

On the morning of 23 January 1948 the services of B Arms breakdown team were urgently required at London Bridge, Central Section. At 9.30 am the electric 8.05 am ex-Seaford/ 7.30 am ex-Ore via Eastbourne, a 12 coach formation of two six car corridor 6 PAN/6 PUL units was allowed to draw up to the inner home signals, where it should have stopped while conflicting movements were completed. The train, however, ran by the signals and at a speed of 15mph collided with the empty coaches of the 8.20 am from Brighton, another 12 coach corridor train standing at platform 14. The latter train was forced over the buffer stops demolishing W. H. Smith's bookstall killing a man standing at the bookstall and injuring 34 passengers. The motorman waiting to take the empties of the 8.20 from Brighton had a narrow escape as did the staff working in the bookstall. The leading cab of the 8.05 from Seaford was bent into a 'vee' and both the motorman and a trainee motorman also in the cab, were so badly injured that they died in their wrecked cab. The cause of the accident was inexplicable as the motorman concerned was regularly in and out of London Bridge. The damaged trains were taken to New Cross Gate down sidings for inspection and B Arms crane and vans tidied up.

As mentioned in the previous chapter, the decision to run-down New Cross Gate motive power depot had been taken before nationalisation and from June 1947 the gradual closure commenced. Men had the choice of transferring to Norwood or Bricklayers Arms. Most drivers elected to go to B Arms while the majority of firemen decided in favour of Norwood. Transfer was on the usual basis of seniority and as soon as vacancies occurred in Nos 1, 2 and 3 links at B Arms they were filled by New Cross men, who at first needed pilot-men on their first trips after a quick look over the roads they were to work on. Whenever possible the new entrants to the Eastern Section main line were given a B Arms driver as pilotman enabling the ex-Gate drivers to get the feel of the road which can only be obtained by actually driving over it, rather than by just watching it. With the Gate men came their engines, with their panting Westinghouse brake pumps. The E3 and E4 0–6–2 tanks, with their inside tool boxes arranged in two layers and looking like the top half of an upright piano, gained the name of 'the piano tanks' by the new hosts under whose roofs they rested. All Brighton engines were at first referred to as 'relics' by B Arms enginemen and fitters. As the integration of duties continued, B Arms drivers found themselves having a pilotman—a New Cross driver, of course—particularly when No 2 link was given the 3.20 am London Bridge to Brighton newspaper train, with an Atlantic. The tip-flap firehole door gave the B Arms firemen a hard time and the 9min allowance from London Bridge to pass Forest Hill was often exceeded. Time was not lost, however, when the Atlantic was manned by an all New Cross crew.

At the end of 1947, the duty was re-diagrammed for a Schools class, which ran the Brighton to Bournemouth service after the paper train. Until that time the biggest 4–4–0 on the Brighton Section was the class B4X (the 'Greyladies') and one of the ex-Gate men to go into No 1 link, Sid Oelman, admitted in front of his colleagues that 'New Cross had nothing like a Schools!' Sid, together with Ted Jakes, became expert handlers of the Schools and because of their style of driving were referred to as 'rubber heeled' drivers ('you could not hear them coming'). While both B Arms and New Cross men found it difficult to adjust to each other's engines, the New Cross men found it more difficult to adapt from their previous bare eight hour days to the nine and ten hour days which were normal at The Brick. Another driver from the Gate to go into No 1 link was George Deacon, an ex-Bournemouth Central man before he migrated to New Cross. He did not link-up the reversing gear as much as the other drivers at The Brick, and Driver Jim Weeks, who lived near Forest Hill station, said he could hear a Schools, with George at the regulator, when it passed Brockley station two miles away!

Among the many drivers who transferred to B Arms were the 'three Brighton Bills'—Bill Day, Bill Halliday and Bill Thompson—so called by B Arms men since they still wore their London, Brighton & South Coast cap badges!

With the enginemen came one of the New Cross running foremen, Percy Molyneaux. The B Arms men wondered about Perce; could he handle the 125 engines stabled at B Arms, do the standard 12 hour foreman's shift, get used to being short of men and quickly master the intricacies of Eastern Section workings? One afternoon, shortly before the rush hour commenced in the depot, an ex-Brighton piano tank, E3 No 2463, had taken coal and her driver, Ted Morey, left her in charge of his young fireman while he found out from Foreman Molyneaux where she was to be berthed. Upon receiving instructions to put her on 5, Old Shed, Driver Morey set the points for the turntable road and told the fireman to take her to the table, the usual privilege given to young and budding stokers. The fireman checked his side and returned to the driving position, on the left hand side of the engine and moved off. Coming towards him was another Brighton tank, No 2460; shouts came from the coal-men, but too late, the two engines met on the points adjacent to the foreman's office, and despite emergency brake applications by both enginemen, were buffer-locked!

The mere whisper of the magic word 'pitch-in' in any loco depot, brought a host of spectators, and B Arms was no exception. The collision had blocked the turntable road, and the Carriage Shed, and engines could not get off the coal road; B Arms was well and truly closed! The fitters arrived and reckoned it would take them an hour to free the engines. Driver Morey's comments to his foreman can well be imagined.

Amidst the advice and fluent remarks, Foreman Molyneaux had a few words with Driver Relph. Perce climbed on to engine 2463 and Driver Relph on to his engine. 2460 was given a little steam forward as did Perce to 2463, then Driver Relph slammed on the brake as Perce put 2463 into reverse with steam still on. The two engines parted with only a slight dent on one of the buffers of No 2463! B Arms was open for business again and all present had to agree that 'that bloke from the Gate was not too bad for a Brighton man'—a compliment indeed. What happened to the young fireman? Well, I am happy to relate that I did not hear another word about this incident!

I have already mentioned the sounds of trains at Forest Hill, at the top of the $2\frac{1}{2}$ mile climb from New Cross Gate. Several B Arms men lived there, and most could tell the time by the class of train heard at various times in the night. At one minute to midnight, an Arthur would rumble through with the 11.50 pm London Bridge to Dover Mail via the Old Road (Redhill and Tonbridge); soon afterwards, the unmistakable sound of a Schools could be heard as she rushed towards London Bridge with the 11 pm ex-Brighton Mail. At 1.10 am another Schools would dash past with the 10.10 pm Dover to Cannon Street Mail, and at 3.32 am the down Brighton paper train would rattle through with the same Schools that had brought up the Mail from Brighton. At 4.40 am, the sharp staccato bark of a C2X 0–6–0 with the 4.15 am B Arms–Tattenham goods, with an E5 banking would rouse the slumbers of the lineside inhabitants of Brockley, Honor Oak Park and Forest Hill. From 12.20 am onwards, double whistles would be heard, informing the signalman at Forest Hill box that the banking engine was waiting at the crossover to return light to New Cross Gate or B Arms as engines had been doing since 1844! The night was never lonely and if the expected train was even a minute late, one suspected that all was not well on the footplate.

About this period (1947–8) an amusing incident occurred which mirrors exactly public standards of decency. At Charing Cross and Cannon Street stations chalk marks appeared on the station walls—not the usual graffiti, but engine stopping marks in relation to the position of the water columns. N15 was for a King Arthur, V for a Schools and so on. Not unnaturally the letters WC indicated the stopping place for a West Country class Pacific. Immediately, the respective stationmasters received complaints from delicate-minded passengers and the letters BOB (Battle of Britain) were substituted and the complaints ceased!

It was customary, when men were available, for No 1 and No 2 link enginemen taking an engine light to London, to be seen away. Like most Southern depots, there was not only a shortage of men but the tools carried on each engine; one bucket, set of spanners, box of detonators, red flags, 2 flare lamps, gauge glass lamp, coal pick, firing shovel, small hammer, long scoop, short scoop (depending on class of engine), dart, rake, three headlamps and three headboard discs, one of which had to carry the engine duty number displayed by stuck-on printed numbers. As many of these necessary items were in short supply, it was sometimes necessary to 'borrow' them from other engines. A few of the more lazy firemen used to remove lighted headlamps from the footplate and other tools which they needed. One morning the engine for the 5.45 am Hastings paper train was seen away for Driver Deacon and his fireman, Len Pritchard. At 6.02 am the train was observed by Inspector Mockeridge, who was waiting on the platform at Orpington station. On arrival at B Arms on one of his frequent visits, Inspector Mockeridge asked Foreman Foote if B Arms had devised a new firing technique for the Schools class and Jim Foote replied 'Not to my knowledge, why?' Mockeridge laughed and related how he had seen Driver Deacon and Fireman Pritchard simultaneously firing 934 *St Lawrence* with head-board discs in lieu of a firing shovel! Someone had removed the engine shovel!

The summer of 1948 was warm, and traffic to the Kent Coast resorts was heavy. Every available engine was pressed into service. Senior passed firemen found themselves booked as drivers of holiday relief trains, many with firemen of little, if any, main line experience.

One Sunday morning, at the height of the summer, the 9.15 am Charing Cross–Dover express had, in place of the usual Schools class, one of B Arms King Arthurs, No 799

Sir Ironside, at the head end. On Sundays only, the 9.15 was fast from Waterloo to Folkestone Central, timed just a shade under the pre-war allowance of 80min from Charing Cross. The load was eleven coaches, and the train was popular with daytrippers to the Kent Coast.

The Arthur was still in Southern Railway livery, and was always kept in a clean condition so that she did credit to the malachite green paint and polished metal-work. *Sir Ironside* had the reputation at B Arms of being a good engine, a compliment indeed coming from B Arms men who generally did not hold the Arthurs in the same high esteem that they had for the Schools. Nevertheless, the four Arthurs shedded at The Brick (794, 795, 798 and 799) were reliable engines and maybe, because there were only four, compared with 18 Schools, enginemen never really got to know them. Only three drivers at B Arms really became Arthur masters, two ex-New Cross Gate men, Sid Oelman and Ted Jakes, and Jack Glew, known as 'Sticky' Glew. Driver Glew was in charge that Sunday morning, and as he sat waiting departure time, indulging in the driver's privileged past-time of watching the passengers entrain, he was amazed to see a strange figure walking up the platform. The man was dressed in blue and white striped denim overalls, a white spotted red kerchief around his neck. On his head was a striped base-ball-style cap and in his mouth was a cigar that was longer than any smoked by Winston Churchill. Jack told his fireman to come and have a look at 'Casey Jones'. The man stopped at the cabside of *Sir Ironside* and produced a footplate pass. He announced that he had just retired after 45 years on the Canadian Pacific Railway, and his colleagues had made a collection which had enabled him to come to England and make his last footplate trips on English locomotives. He then, most respectfully, asked Driver Glew if he could come aboard.

Jack Glew was one of B Arms improvement class instructors and coached many firemen to pass out as drivers. Jack's knowledge of the intricacies of the vacuum brake were his speciality, while his knowledge of rules and enginemanship were hard to surpass. In a few sentences Jack conveyed to the visiting Canadian engineer the differences of English engines to his own and explained the signals, too. At 9.15 the right away was given by the guard and No 799 moved easily away from Charing Cross, to stop at Waterloo. It was essential to get the fire well alight under the door on an Arthur, and this was best achieved by using the half door plate—similar to the draw-plate or Dutch oven on a Schools. To use the full door on an Arthur simply pulled the fire to pieces and the art of firing an Arthur was to keep a sloping fire, with the back corners and under the door well alight. Once clear of Waterloo, the fire was bright all over and the first seven shovelfuls were swung into the firebox. Driver Glew sounded the whistle as *Sir Ironside* approached No 3 road through London Bridge station, and with the reverser on 30 per cent and the regulator fully open in the first port, the 9.15 pounded through the station at the maximum permitted speed of 30mph.

The Canadian Engineer, whose name was Bill, stood behind Jack Glew, his cigar unlit; passing on each side were the numerous electric trains to which he gave a quick glance, then his eyes were back on the road. Approaching North Kent East, another seven shovelfuls went in, the exhaust injector was on and the needle of the pressure gauge quivered on 200; New Cross was $\frac{1}{2}$ mile ahead and a further seven shovelfuls were swung into the glaring fire. Jack pointed to the whistle chain and Bill gave what he afterwards described as a double-pull as 799 thundered through New Cross. The Canadian grinned like a schoolboy as the sound of the East-leigh whistle blasted the morning air and warned passengers to stand well back, please. The fireman gave the 'open palm' hand signal to the driver to indicate that St Johns starter was green and at 45mph the 9.15 swung under the Nunhead flyover and started the climb towards Knockholt. Driver Glew moved the reverser forward to 40 per cent and the fireman put on another round of coal. The noise from the engine's exhaust echoed across the deserted Lewisham High Road below and with the boiler pressure on 195, Hither Green was passed at 45mph. At Grove Park the reverser was moved back to 30 per cent and Jack put her into the 'big valve' ie opened the regulator wide; by Elmstead Woods the reverser was back to 25 per cent and the Arthur was purring like a cat. Bill was fascinated by the four track way and shouted that, back home, much of the main line was single track. The Arthur rocked over Petts Wood junction, where the spur from the Chatham main line converges and with the pressure at 200 and the injector still on, the opportunity was taken to spray the tender. Just outside Orpington, the fireman fired again, and then took up position to watch the road ahead. 'Control' was just ahead and the usual black-raincoated figure in a bowler hat indicated that an inspector was watching the engine and its crew. Had an inspector been available, one would have travelled on the footplate of *Sir Ironside* as was the custom when a visitor was present on the footplate, but Bill was unaccompanied on that particular trip. Bill sounded the whistle as the 9.15 swept through Orpington, the fireman guided him to his side of the footplate for another B Arms custom—that of waving to the nurses down in Orpington Hospital! By Chelsfield speed had dropped to 40mph and the summit of the long climb from St Johns about $\frac{1}{4}$ mile beyond Knockholt was passed at a shade under 40. Downhill now, and *Sir Ironside* accelerated into Polhill tunnel whistle screaming, to emerge at a steady 60mph to sweep through Dunton Green with steam almost shut off, the fire shimmering bright and with the blower on a quarter of a turn to stop any chance of a blow-back. The Canadian visitor held on to the grab-rail as the Arthur was gently checked by a slight brake application to keep the speed down to the prescribed 60mph speed limit between the signalbox outside Sevenoaks and the London end of Sevenoaks tunnel, a restriction still in force today.

Sir Ironside again accelerated on the drop through the tunnel (at 3,453yd the longest on the Southern) and speed had increased to almost 80mph as it emerged but had to be checked to 75 to pass Hildenborough, and soon afterwards to a shade over 40 to negotiate the sharp left-hand curve into Tonbridge, which was passed on the through road. As soon as the engine passed under the road bridge, Glew opened the regulator wide, and with the cut-off on 40 per cent, No 799 picked up speed to pass Paddock Wood at a good 60mph. At this point Driver Glew stood to one side and said to the Canadian Engineer 'She's all yours, chum'. Bill took the regulator and varied the cut-off slightly.

Passing Marden, No 799 was touching 75 and Ashford was passed on the dot, right on time. The Canadian enjoyed tea from the tea-can, stewed to perfection on the mantelshelf over the firehole door and the only time that he looked a little worried was at the approach to Shakespeare tunnel, with its very narrow portals, but Driver Glew assured him that the engine and its train go through easily enough, but one's head and elbows should be inside the cab! At Dover, the guest left the footplate to have a wash and brush-up before joining a Stewarts Lane crew for a trip back to Victoria on a boat train.

As was customary at the height of the summer traffic, No 4 link jobs were covered by passed firemen, acting as drivers, allowing the drivers to run specials. In 1948, one very fine morning, passed fireman Cyril Young was in charge of the 3.08 am empties to Cannon Street, before running light to London Bridge to take the 4.50 am Old Road newspaper train to Margate. The empty train had attached to it two bogie-bolsters from the engineer's department at New Cross Gate which were to be used for track-work at Cannon Street. The train, with Schools class 934 running tender first, had just passed Peak Frean's biscuit factory, surrounded as always with the delicious aroma of freshly baked biscuits, when the early morning stillness was broken by what at first appeared to be a sudden, violent thunderstorm, with brilliant displays of lightning which ran up and down the train, the leading vehicle of which (a bogie-bolster) was on fire. Since water could not be used in the vicinity of live rails, Driver Young ran smartly into London Bridge station, where a chemical extinguisher put out the small fire. The guard examined the rest of the train and finding nothing amiss, it proceeded to Cannon Street. Young and his fireman worked the 4.50 as far as Ashford and returned with the 8.31 (7.03 am ex-Margate) to Cannon Street, being relieved at London Bridge. Waiting with their relief was Inspector Mockeridge who informed them that the first electric train from Dartford that morning had come to a standstill near Peak Freans owing to the displacement of the conductor rail.

An inquiry was soon forthcoming at Waterloo and the enginemen's alteration sheet advised Young and his mate to go 'passenger to W'loo to attend inquiry'—an ominous entry. Assembled at Waterloo were a long line of men—guards, shunters, yard foremen, signalmen, carriage and wagon examiners, two porters from London Bridge, a permanent way inspector, the motorman and guard of the electric train and the B Arms enginemen. A head office clerk called out the names of the assembled men and a voice called out that two people had not been called. The clerk enquired the names of the missing people and got the reply 'His Majesty King George and Jane Russell' (then showing at the Old Kent Road Picture House in the film *The Outlaw*). The clerk hastily withdrew into his office amid roars of laughter. The inquiry, ably conducted by T. E. Chrimes and F. L. Howard and assisted by several other officers, lasted all day and each waiting witness was given 2s to buy lunch in the staff canteen. The blame for the incident was laid on the guard of the train, who should have ensured that the bolster chains were properly secured before departing from Rother-hithe Road. The loose chains had pulled out the insulators carrying the live rail, causing the lightning which had caused the wagon to catch fire.

Throughout the summer, the many extra race specials made the job of the list clerk to provide extra engine crews, more trying. B Arms covered the Margate and Ramsgate excursions as well as the Hastings run, and it was on this route that most lost time was experienced. The severe gradients and curving nature of the route was a trial for enginemen regularly running over the Hastings branch, for passed firemen acting as drivers, were generally given a very junior fireman as mate and this did not encourage good time-keeping by virtue of the fact that the driver very often had to take a turn with the shovel to keep a reasonable head of steam. In the summer all specials carried in addition to their normal duty number displayed on the headcode disc, a timekeeping number (usually the working timetable train number) on a rectangular board, tied very firmly to the smokebox-door. These timekeeping boards were for the benefit of signalmen to give priority or secondary paths in the event of the train running late. Boat trains had Q timings (Q being the letter used to denote paths for trains run when required) on an alternative route—for example an up boat train booked via Tonbridge would also have a provisional path via Maidstone East and vice versa, in case of late running.

To illustrate one of the harder trips commonplace during the summer traffic, let us join a B Arms crew on the 9.06 am relief express to Hastings. It was booked to call at Waterloo, London Bridge, fast to Sevenoaks, Tonbridge, Tunbridge Wells, St Leonards and Hastings. The train consisted of ten of Maunsell's narrow bodied 8ft wide coaches, including a refreshment car. On the morning in question, the enginemen were not pleased to have engine No 1783, an L1, which was the black sheep of B Arms, having more lost time to her discredit than any other engine of her class. For some unknown reason she was a very shy steamer on most of her runs, and not at all a popular engine! The coal on her tender was the usual 1948 mixture of Kent dust and small soft coal with probably a small residue of coal block briquette dust; add to those ingredients Driver Luxford's fireman, a lad who had spent the previous six weeks as fireman on shunting engines! As mentioned earlier, the L1 was not any fireman's engine, as they needed very careful firing to

Right: Driver's view from the footplate of 2-6-0 No 31893 as it climbs Herne Bay bank.

Author

Below: Class L 4-4-0 No 1776 heads through Shortlands with a London–Kent Coast express. These engines were the mainstay of express services all over Kent and until the building of the Schools 4-4-0s nothing larger was allowed on the Tonbridge–Hastings line. At various times B Arms crews worked 'rounder' turns going down from London via Tonbridge and Dover to Ramsgate and back up via the Chatham route to London.

C. R. L. Coles

The Schools class 4-4-0s, so beloved by Bricklayers Arms crews not only on their regular Hastings turns but for any express work: *above*, No 30937 *Epsom* a large chimney engine, waits to leave Charing Cross for Hastings in summer 1958; *below*, No 30908 with the original small chimney, coasts through St Johns with a Hastings–Charing Cross train on 4 June 1957. In the background is the bridge which was destroyed in the St Johns collision in the following December.

I. S. Carr

bring out the best in them, and No 1783 was not the best one of her class.

At 9.06 am the right away was given by the guard and off they went, with steam whimpering at the safety valves at the full working pressure of 180lb/sq in. After the stop at Waterloo, Driver Luxford opened out the L1 and arrived at London Bridge with 160lb on the clock and the injector singing away. By then, the train was crowded, and the fireman shut off the injector to bring her round. Driver Luxford looked at his mate's fire and suggested a quick rake through. The blower was on a full turn and by the time they received the right away No 1783 had 170lb pressure and half a glass of water, that is the water was half way up the gauge glass.

With the cut-off on 30 per cent they hurried over the arches and by North Kent East signalbox, the train was moving at about 45mph. With the injector on the pressure was, however, moving slowly backwards and passing New Cross was already down to 160. Luxford eased the regulator, and shortened the cut-off to 25 per cent, pressure remained at 160, but at the next station, St Johns, the real hard work had only just begun. It was a warm morning and the sweat was already running down the fireman's face although they had only been running about 10min! By Hither Green, pressure had fallen to 155lb, and Driver Luxford gave the fire some personal attention. On the 1 in 140 gradient approaching Elmstead Woods, only 150lb was on the clock. Luxford eased the regulator passing Orpington, where the gradient levels out to 1 in 310, but the injector had to be kept on as the water level was only an inch above the bottom of the gauge glass with the regulator open! If only they could pass the summit at Knockholt. . . . Driver Luxford again fired No 1783 and the fireman, who felt that he was not earning his keep, scrambled into the tender and combed down some decent bits of hard coal. The next two miles at 1 in 120 was touch and go, mortgaging water for steam then steam for water, but in spite of the crew's efforts as Chelsfield station was reached, with just 125lb of steam, No

1783 made an unscheduled stop as the vacuum-brake leaked on, just by Chelsfield signalbox. There then followed the following dialogue:

Signalman: 'You can't stop here'.

Driver: 'We have'.

Signalman: 'The 9.15 is not far behind you'.

Driver: '. . . . the 9.15'.

Signalman—unabashed by the un-friendly tone of the sweating Driver: 'The 9.25 Hastings is behind the 9.15'.

Driver: 'Ditto to the 9.25'.

This delightful cross-talk act was interrupted by the appearance of the guard, who, blissfully unaware of the fore-going conversation, jovially enquired 'Has the engine's spring run down?'—the fireman's reply was totally unprintable but the guard saved the day by stating that 'No 1783 has lost more time than I have had hot dinners'. Tension eased, Luxford went into the signalbox, signed the train register and the signalman telephoned Tonbridge Loco for 'a pull to the Wells for a sick engine'.

After 9min, with the 9.15 held at Orpington, and the 9.25 creeping slowly between Chislehurst and Petts Wood, No 1783 had revived herself and with 170lb on the pressure gauge and half a glass of water, she restarted her train and after the scheduled Sevenoaks stop, reached Tonbridge about 22min late. Here, Tonbridge Loco provided a pilot engine for the steep climb up to Tunbridge Wells. The pilot was a class D Coppertop, No 1733 and her crew were delighted to have to go on a B Arms special! Smart coupling up and quick brake test were completed within 2min, and with steam roaring from her safety valves the Coppertop piloted No 1783 up the steep 1 in 47 climb towards Tunbridge Wells. The Tonbridge driver thrashed 1733 all the way and with some assistance from 1783, something like sectional time was maintained. The Tonbridge fireman kept his engine well round for steam so well that she had steam to spare and blew-off vigorously as they left Tunbridge Wells Station; unfortunately No 1733 was priming, water entered the brake valve and the cavalcade came to a standstill a quarter mile past Tunbridge Wells Station! All in all it had not been a very good morning.

Up to 1952, a regular top link duty at B Arms was the 4.32 pm to Ramsgate via Swanley, first stop Rochester; an L1 was the usual motive power for this Cannon Street business train. When engine No 1783 was on this duty, Farningham Road was passed at the usual 75mph gallop but with no water in the bottom of the gauge glass and both injectors on and the fireman hard at it all the way!

Drama was not confined to the footplate, however, as any running foreman would hasten to tell you. The men in the yard had their moments, too. Almost at the end of the summer in 1948, Foreman Fred Sos Gregson was on the afternoon shift at B Arms. The time was mid-afternoon, and the coal road was, as usual, full of engines. The coal was mostly slack and the coalmen were loading the little ½-ton coal skips as fast as they could. Two Brighton E3 piano tanks were coaled in succession and much of the coal had fallen into the four-foot way behind them. The next engine to take coal was a West Country Pacific, which moved off after taking some eight skips of coal. Suddenly shouts of 'Whoa, whoa' from the coalmen—the driver smartly dropped the brake handle, but too late, the first two wheels of the bogie had been derailed by piled-up coal. The driver climbed down from his cab and headed straight towards the chargeman coalman. Foreman Gregson arrived between the two men. The driver and coalman spoke at the same time and Gregson calmly puffed at his pipe. Charlie Richford and the break-down boys arrived on the scene together with George Clark, standing in for H. Packham who was on leave.

When the two men had calmed down, Gregson waved away the breakdown gang and led the driver back to his engine and climbed up into the cab with him. Foreman Gregson gently reversed the spam and she rerailed herself over the pile of crushed coal that had caused the derailment in the first place.

Gregson, still puffing at his pipe, left the cab and in a few quietly spoken but well-chosen words told the coaling charge-hand to clear the four-foot way and within 2min had returned to his little office.

Most B Arms men complained at the antiquated method of coaling used at their depot. Coal was shovelled out of 20-ton coal wagons into the $\frac{1}{2}$-ton skips which were hoisted up over the engine; only two locomotives could be coaled at one time. By contrast—and what a contrast—at Ramsgate a huge hopper there held about 100 tons of coal which could fill an empty West Country tender in two minutes flat! Invariably, enginemen remained on the footplate to watch the operation, but were eventually forbidden to do so. Shortly afterwards the hopper got jammed in the open position and buried a King Arthur.

5

Visitors, Coppertops, and goods trains

Charing Cross, on a Saturday morning was one of the favourite spots for locomotive enthusiasts of all ages. As at all termini, enginemen were generally pleased to answer questions about their engines and railway matters in general. Youngsters, clutching their spotters notebooks and reference books could be seen standing at the end of the main line platforms, exchanging information with each other and sometimes asking the enginemen whether the home depot of a particular engine was Dover or Ramsgate, and then having got the information 'from the driver's mouth' lauding it over their fellow spotters!

Then there were the fathers, lifting their youngsters up to footplate height 'to look at the lovely fire' and of course having a good look themselves. If there was no loco inspector about, many drivers would take a long look at the child and ask 'Would you like to come up and have a good look?' Rarely would a child refuse, and once aboard father was forgotten, as most children dream to be on an engine. More often than not, the sheer disappointment of not being asked showed on father's face and tactfully a driver would enquire if the child would be all right on its own or would the father like to come up as well—just to look after it. Of course, it was strictly against the rules for any unauthorised person to get on to the footplate without a footplate permit, but many a footplate career has been motivated by an invitation to 'come up'. I well remember being lifted on to the footplate of a King Arthur at Waterloo, by a kindly driver, when I was just six years old. It was an experience that was never forgotten and one has only to close one's eyes to recall the huge fire, the smell of warm oil, steam and Welsh coal.

One bright, sunny morning at Charing Cross, Driver Bill Snell was waiting time on the 8.25 am to Hastings. A few minutes before starting time, a tall, grey haired gentleman and his attractive daughter, stood gazing into the cab of 933 *Kings Canterbury* (later renumbered 30933). Bill invited them both on to the footplate and started to point out one or two things which he thought might interest them. The daughter pointed to the small ejector on the brake valve and commenced to name all the controls from left to right, finishing up with the front and back damper controls on the fireman's side. The gentleman thanked Bill, gave him half-a-crown and the pair stepped down, the girl smiling sweetly. We never did find out just who they were, but Bill was of the opinion that attendance at improvement classes would fill the canteen if she paid it a visit! Years later, I met Bill again and he was still going on about that incident.

Passed Fireman Harry Bishop and his fireman were on 913 *Christ's Hospital* at the head of a holiday relief train from Charing Cross to Dover one morning. A smart young gent kept walking up and down past the engine and Bishop was not surprised when the man stopped at the cabside, touching it almost reverently: 'My old school, you know' he said, 'my name is Knight'. Harry, by no means a chess fan, could not resist extending his grimy hand and replying 'Bishop—now that makes us old school chums!'

A little earlier in the year, while in the top link, Bishop was firing the 5.00 pm from Cannon Street. The engine, a spam, was priming rather badly and water entered the vacuum brake, bringing the train to a stand in Orpington station, at the height of the evening rush hour. While his driver blew the brake off, with the big ejector ('shoving the 'andle right up' was the correct term), Bishop took the opportunity of getting some cool, fresh air out of the cab side window. On the platform, an upright, military looking gentleman, walked over to Bishop, his umbrella in one hand and a gold time-piece in the other:

Gent: 'Why have you stopped here, my man?'

Fireman Bishop: 'She won't go, governor'.

The gent pointed to her nameplate: 'She's a brand new Battle of Britain class, man'.

Bishop: 'She still won't go, governor'.

Gent: 'Damn it all, man, she bears the name *Hurricane*'.

'Ah, yes' replied Bishop as the train began to move, 'I rather think that's what we needs behind us to make up time'.

During 1949, many foreign (ie other regions) technical visitors rode on Southern footplates as part of the inter-regional exchange of ideas and information. For B Arms men to have guests on the footplate, was nothing new. From time to time, various people who had managed to obtain a much sought after footplate pass, had ridden with the men from The Brick and received from them explanations, tolerance and the traditional footplate hospitality of sharing the tea-can en route. At the end of the run, the name of the nearest and best public house was revealed to thirsty guests and it was not unknown for the enginemen to accept an invitation to have a pint with them.

In general, visitors on the footplate were accompanied by an inspector and almost without exception, the guests thoroughly enjoyed themselves. At the risk of over-stressing the point, there had to be a very good reason to ride on the footplate. Indeed, management frowned on enginemen riding on the footplate when they were not part of the train crew, or riding in the cab of an electric train, other than when they were learning the road. The presence of an extra person in the cab could distract the driver. Nevertheless, many men who left the comradeship of the locomotive cab for the lonely life of an electric-train driver, still liked to have a colleague who had just finished duty or was on his way to start work, to ride with him in the cab. From past experience when riding up front, both men by instinct watch the road ahead while they are talking. Many a keen fireman has ridden up front, instead of on the cushions, and gained useful extra road knowledge in the process, particularly at spots where the nature of the road called for him to be firing.

One visitor, however, is unlikely to forget a trip he had with B Arms men on No 920 *Rugby,* one summer morning in 1949. Because of a shortage of locomotive inspectors, this particular guest was unaccompanied and no doubt, since he was a technical man from another region, it was thought to be unnecessary to accompany him anyway.

Driver Joe Bond was somewhat surprised when, at 9.10, a man climbed on to the footplate at Charing Cross. He did not ask if he could come aboard, let alone show a footplate pass. I should mention here that even inspectors, who had every right to ride on the footplate, diplomatically asked the driver if he minded having him ride with him; the request could not be refused, but the courtesy was always appreciated. Joe Bond asked, in plain Anglo-Saxon, who the intruder thought he was. The man then announced that he was a technical man from the . . . . region, and that on his region engines really moved. He went on to say that this run down on the 9.15 was really only a long shunt! The 9.15, on a Sunday morning, was fast from Waterloo to Folkestone Central in 83min—not a too difficult timing, but in 1949, a maximum speed limit of 75mph was the rule of the day, so that one could not take too much advantage of the Tonbridge to Ashford race track.

Joe told the visitor to stand just behind him, which placed him just above the trailing coupled wheel arch, where he (the visitor) would find it unnecessary to hold on to the grab-rail during the shunt to Folkestone! Driver Bond omitted to mention that *Rugby* was due for her visit to the shops, that her driving wheels were down to about 6ft 5in or that her casing was about half an inch away from the cab—when standing still. *Rugby* was still painted in Southern Railway livery of malachite green, with engine number in gold, and though she was ready for her overhaul, she could really go, as we had discovered on a Guinness Brewery special from Margate to Victoria the previous week, when by Bromley South 920 was running 6min early on the non-stop special. One thing was certain, *Rugby* was riding a little rough, as our guest was soon to find out, and since she was a B Arms engine which had a reputation for being able to do 'half an hour in twenty-five minutes', we were more than pleased when the guard gave us the right away. By the time we had reached North Kent East, *Rugby* was touching 50mph and swaying beautifully as she took the gentle right hand curve outside New Cross; then she dropped smartly down on her right-hand side, tossing her visitor upwards, who grabbed at the cab-rail just as she straightened out after yawing to her left, whereupon the footplate dropped from beneath the visitor's feet and then kicked him as she rose up and levelled off. Joe yelled to him that 'We're still going uphill' as he eased the bridle-rod forward to 35 per cent. The sudden noise as the 9.15 tore through New Cross brought the guest back to reality and he resumed his hands behind his back stance. The sharp right hand curve at St Johns, however, shot him across to the fireman's side of the footplate, where he took the opportunity of taking a breath of fresh air away from the slip-stream of Joe Bond's pungent pipe smoke.

By Orpington, the 9.15 was one minute up and with the lever still on 30 per cent *Rugby* was chirruping along merrily, and upon emerging from Polhill tunnel was doing 75, with only 100lb of steam showing on the steam chest pressure gauge out of the 220 showing on her boiler pressure gauge. The prescribed whistle for a $\frac{1}{4}$ mile on entering Sevenoaks tunnel added to the clamour of the whirling coupling and connecting rods and by the time the guest had endured a further $\frac{1}{4}$ mile of whistling in the centre of the tunnel and yet another at the exit, his ears were ringing as *Rugby* streaked down through The Weald, past Hildenborough at slightly above the prescribed limit. After slowing for the Tonbridge curve, Joe informed the guest that we were about to start running! From 40 per cent cut-off through Tonbridge Joe progressively wound back the bridle-rod until passing Staplehurst it was back to 15 per cent and *Rugby* was swaying like a small boat in the wake of an ocean liner. Joe and I enjoyed sips of tea en route but did not offer any to the visitor, who was clinging grimly to the cab-rail as he stood over that trailing coupled axle. The Schools was in fine fettle and when the guest was asked if he wished to have a go on the shovel, a sickly smile showed that he dare not leave that grab-rail!

Driver Bond took great pains to draw the visitor's attention to the 140lb pressure in the steam chest, showing the engine's well-designed front-end as *Rugby* touched the 80 mark with her 11-coach train, as the arrow-straight track flashed beneath us. More sips of tea for the driver and fireman as *Rugby* ate up the miles. Her pitch and yaw movement was making a sickly impression on the guest, who looked most unhappy. Had our guest, been more sociable, he would have been given the fireman's seat to sit on and not been subjected to the swaying that a standing person, trying to keep their balance, suffers. When he left the footplate at Folkestone Central, Joe leaned down to him and said 'Though we are a small railway with small engines we do move 'em along when we're shunting!'

During 1949, the West Country and Battle of Britain engines were re-numbered in the 34000 range—21C 170 became 34070; this class of engine became a regular performer on the Sunday 9.15 am down. When the general line speed limit was raised to 85mph, several drivers decided to find out just what the spams were capable of. A few weeks after the foreign visitor episode, Driver Bond and myself were again at the head of the Sunday 9.15 down. The 85mph limit was common knowledge not only to enginemen but to enthusiasts as well, who, by using rail-joint or $\frac{1}{4}$-milepost method and the second hand of a watch could observe and record train speeds. It has often been noted that members of the clergy have, through the years, shown a keen interest in railway matters and that their impartial efforts at timing trains has generally proved to be reliable, frank and honest.

On the morning in question, after being delayed by engineering work near Sevenoaks, costing us about 4min, this was an excuse for the driver to make up time (observing such local speed restrictions as were in force at the time). 34077 was a Ramsgate engine, and once past Tonbridge, she was given her head. I was much too busy even to attempt any timing. Joe had really got her running on her springs, steady as a rock. The boiler pressure varied between 240 and 265lb, which was normal and ample for any train, and saved her from blowing off if the regulator had to be closed for adverse signals. The steam chest pressure gauge was showing just 140lb—half her working pressure. The driver was enthused by the engine's performance and yelled out to me that 'the telegraph poles are going by so fast that they look like iron railings on a churchyard wall!' By Folkestone Central, we had not only regained our lost 4min but picked up 1min on the timing. As we stood at Folkestone Central, a rather excited clergyman came up to the engine-cab. In his hands were a board with two stop watches mounted on it. The vicar smiled or perhaps beamed is a better word, and Joe invited him up on the footplate. 'Wonderful run, driver, wonderful run—do you realise that you were doing 94mph at Head-corn?' Joe said that he thought she was moving-on just a bit. Bearing in mind the 85mph speed limit, the vicar added 'I only hope that you do not have to go and see your governor, that's all'. Joe replied, very promptly: 'That's all right, your reverence—just so long as I don't have to go before your governor, just yet!' The vicar had a good laugh at that reply and was offered a drink of tea from the tea-can, which he accepted. He was delighted to stay on the footplate with us to Dover, and took a turn on the shovel! Joe remarked to the vicar 'As long as you do not end up as a stoker, vicar, I'm sure He won't mind—just this once'.

During 1948, rest days were introduced after the intro-duction of a 44-hour week. No duties could be rostered for just four hours, so that the men had to do four hours overtime to cover a duty. Eventually, it was agreed that each man should have one day off a fortnight (on the front shift). Unfortunately, with the acute shortage of footplatemen, it was virtually impossible for the men to take their day-off unless they had a good reason! As before, the change-over from front shift (12.05 am to 11.55 am sign on) to back shift was done on a Sunday. Rest day coverage, resulted in No 4 link covering No 2 link duties and No 3 covering No 1 link, so that the lower links got a sample of higher link duties.

No 4 link, was a bit of all sorts, relieving at London, taking empties to Rotherhithe Road and Grove Park, taking empties to London and preparing the engine for the main line crew to take her over and so on. Another duty was that of the Bexleyheath pilot. After preparing a Pacific at Ewer Street, the No 4 link men were relieved by Ramsgate men in Ewer Street, at 6.30 pm, for the 7.15 down. The B Arms men would then adjourn to 'The Hop Pole' public house for cheese rolls and light refreshment. At 7 pm they relieved a pair of their own men on a C class 0–6–0 at Ewer Street, from where they ran light to Bexleyheath. The C would romp along at a steady 40 to 50mph, and it was the custom for driver and fireman to exchange places; the fire was made up at Ewer Street, and rarely needed attention on the run down, giving the driver and fireman a welcome breath of fresh air after the high cab temperature of a 4–6–2.

In the top link, in 1948, was Driver George 'Mechanical Colossus' Melville. George was a good driver, but one who always expected a full boiler pressure at all times. For some time, his fireman was Jack 'Popeye' Davis. George used to reckon that 'Popeye' was 'on the floor' (short of steam) with a Schools if the boiler pressure was below 210lb (out of 220). George used to tell his fellow drivers that he liked to see the needle well round on the designed pressure and that he could not stand these '180 touch firemen'. One day Pop Davis recalled how George bet him 10s that on a semi-fast to Dover, he could not keep the boiler at 215 and nothing less but never let the engine blow off! Fireman Davis managed to satisfy these stringent terms of the bet as far as Folkestone, but the train was held by signals in Folkestone Warren for 3min and blew off steam. Melville's reply was 'I knew you couldn't do it' and collected 10s from his fireman there and then.

In No 2 link was a driver whose pallid complexion gave rise to his unfortunate nickname of 'Death'. 'Death' Harvey was an excellent driver, who later on gave O. S. Nock an electrifying run on a Schools. His usual method of restarting a Schools was to place the cut-off in neutral with steam on and move the reverser gently forward until, as he put it, 'the engine found her stride'. He handled a Schools as if he had one as a pet. Some years later I fired to him on a stopping train to Brighton via the Bluebell line, with a class U 2–6–0. With only six South Eastern Birdcage coaches behind us, the U made light of the run and on arrival at Brighton he commented that if we had had a Brighton engine, we would have been lucky to have left Sheffield Park, such was his opinion of Brighton engines.

Our return train was the 11.00 pm up Brighton mail, known by all and sundry as 'the courting couples express'. Officially the mail did not carry passengers, but since coaching stock overhauled at the Lancing carriage works, was attached to this train, it was the done thing to allow people who had missed the last electric train back to town to ride in it. The coaching stock was not on passenger service, however, and was therefore unlit—hence the nickname. That night, Brighton Loco had coaled the Schools for this train with the only coal available—household kitchen nuts! The train called at Haywards Heath, Redhill and East Croydon, then fast to London Bridge, and firing her with kitchen nuts was something akin to throwing paper on the fire; the shovel was never out of my hands until East Croydon. Driver Harvey thought it comical to see a fireman working like a slave on the Brighton line!

For some time, Running Foreman George Clark had stood in for H. Packham by signing privilege ticket orders, sorting out the day to day problems and interviewing men reporting in. It was the practice that any man who failed to arrive for his rostered turn of duty, could come in late and be put in the as required pool. A man who did not present himself for duty, was put down as sick and then had to report in the day before he wished to resume work. One had to report in person to see George Clark and explain the reason for not reporting for duty at the prescribed time (usual excuse—overslept). Once the foreman was satisfied that the man was fit for duty, the man had to tell the list clerk and be informed by him of his duty-number and signing on time, if different from his rostered turn. The official reason for reporting in was to ensure that the man was in fact fit for duty. This method prevented a man taking the day off as he could not go anywhere until he had reported in, so that much of the day was wasted. A man who failed to report in the same day had to come in the next and in so doing lost two days work and since it was very much a case of no work, no pay—even for genuine cases of sickness supported by a doctor's certificate—absenteeism was kept to a minimum.

Pay day at The Brick was a Friday; the visiting pay clerk paid-out from 10.30 am until 1 pm and then again from 2 pm until 6 pm. A man on night duty or 12.05 am therefore had to come back to the depot after he had gone home or write out a pay bearer slip and get one of his colleagues to draw his pay for him. Many of the unmarried firemen, however, did not bother to come in to draw their pay on the Friday or even for one week or two. The form was then to go into George Clark's office and request him to get their money out of the safe. One fireman got George to get his last week's pay out for him. George grumbled as he was trying to put supplements into the new engineman's working timetables piled high on his desk. George slammed the safe shut after the fireman had signed for his pay and turned to resume his mammoth task. The fireman casually requested his pay for the week before the last. George bellowed at the fireman. The fireman repeated his request in answer to which George hurled a pile of engine workings with and without supplements at the fireman, who beat a hasty retreat out of the door. Poor old George then got down on the floor to sort out the result of his temper. Suddenly, by his hands appeared a pair of polished shoes. Without bothering to look up George shouted 'What do you want, your . . . . . last weeks wages, too?' The well modulated voice of F. L. Howard, then London East Divisional Superintendent, replied 'No, George, but I think you really ought to use your desk instead of kneeling on the floor!' Poor old Clarkie went a sort of purple as the fireman who was the cause of his anger returned to request his week's wages before the last to which Clarkie replied—in front of Mr Howard—'Certainly, my son', though the look which the fireman received was, to say the least, most unfatherly. George recovered his composure by the time Mr Howard left and returned to his task. Driver Snell, who had been off sick then entered George Clark's office and gave in his medical certificate from his doctor. Clarkie was very short sighted and looked closely at the doctor's writing. 'So that's what you've had, Bill'. Bill said that he did not know that foremen were trained to read upside-down and turned the certificate the right way up in Clarkie's hand. Once again the air was full of flying engine workings and supplements! Clark retired in 1950.

Drivers who reached retiring age (65) or came off the main line because of failing eyesight, went into a link known as the tankie gang, the duties of which were either shunting trucks in No 3 yard or empty coaches at Rotherhithe Road. The latter duties were carried out with H class 0–4–4 tanks, of which Bricklayers Arms had 11, Nos 1162, 1278, 1309, 1324, 1326, 1500, 1533, 1541, 1542, 1544 and 1546. The H tanks, with their steam-reverse, were ideal engines for carriage shunting—powerful, with a good field of view. Rotherhithe Road was laid out on right-hand curves, so that the driver could see the hand signals from the shunters almost all the time, from his position on the right-hand side of the engine. The H class, however, had a short straight bar regulator, which made it necessary for the driver to be constantly diving in and out of the cab. To obviate this, the fitters at B Arms had devised an extension arm for the regulator, secured by two wing nuts. In rainy weather, the fireman would wrap a cab-sheet around the driver and tie it to the inside of the cab, thereby protecting most of the driver from the rain, but isolating him from the inside of the cab.

One of the tankie gang's (referred to by the firemen as the old man's gang) leading members was Driver Wales. Wales was a portly, red-faced man with a watch-chain across his vast waist-coat. His grease-top hat was highly polished as was his engineman's badge. Every new fireman he would greet with the same preamble: 'So you want to be an engine driver and learn everything about engines, eh?' to which the inevitable reply was, 'Yes', whereupon Wales would thrust the oil-can into the lad's hands and direct him to oil every part of the motion, watching every move the fireman made and seeing every cork was replaced firmly.

However, in the early hours one morning, at Rotherhithe Road sidings, whilst Driver Wales, encased in his cab-sheet to protect him from the driving rain, was busily making up a train of coaches, his fireman nodded off to sleep. Under normal circumstances at Rotherhithe Road the fireman nodding off would not have been of great importance, but on this particular morning, had the fireman remained awake just a few minutes longer he would have heard one of the wing nuts holding the extension shaft to the regulator, fall on to the footplate. Wales got the steady green hand-signal from the shunter to slow down, and he closed his end of the regulator handle. The H however, puffed steadily on, her regulator still open. Wales tried to get into the cab but almost strangled himself on the tightly tied cab-sheet. He yelled to the fireman who was, without doubt, deep in the arms of Morpheous. Driver Wales put No 1324 into reverse just as he got the red light from the shunter, dropping the brake handle at the same time, alas, too late. There was a loud bang as the H tank hit the rake of coaches, and another yell from Driver Wales as the tea-can emptied its precious contents over his feet! After a few well-chosen words to his mate, Wales sent the fireman down to the all-night café in Rotherhithe Road, and by the time he had returned it was 2 am and the shunters had gone to breakfast. Wales took the oppor-

Hop-pickers specials: *above*, 'Use anybody's stock but your own' was obviously in mind when Class E1 4-4-0 No 31067 worked a train of LMR coaches on a London Bridge–Maidstone West hop-pickers train seen here at Yalding on 11 September 1960. *Below*, on similar duty the same month was Class C 0-6-0 No 31693 at Wateringbury.

Derek Cross

Freight on the South Eastern main line: *above*, un-named King Arthur 4-6-0 No 30797 approaches Petts Wood with an up parcels train for London Bridge. *Below*, Class N 2-6-0 No 31873 climbs towards the newly realigned Petts Wood Junction with a down freight from Hither Green and is overtaken by a diesel-electric multiple-unit from Charing Cross to Hastings in June 1959.

Derek Cross

tunity of looking at the front-end of No 1324 to see if there was any damage, while his fireman climbed up into the cab, which was filled with smoke. The fireman turned on the blower to clear the air and just caught sight of Driver Wales's bacon, egg and fried bread fly-off the firing shovel and into the firebox! Driver Wales's comments are best left to the reader's imagination. His mate made yet another trip to the all-night café to buy bacon and egg sandwiches to placate his driver. Shunting at Rotherhithe Road was never really dull! Driver Wales retired in 1947 and lived another 25 years in happy retirement.

In contrast, shunting at Willow Walk, was hard work for the fireman, who had to keep a sharp look-out all the time. Naturally, shunting at Willow Walk was carried out with Brighton engines—an E3 or E4 or an E1, called rooters by B Arms men, though to a New Cross man a rooter was an A1X, the diminutive Stroudley 0–6–0Ts. One night on the Willow Walk pilot duty was E1 0–6–0T No 2151. This engine had a leaking stay in her firebox, which did not matter shunting up and down the yard. Around 1.30 in the morning, there was a lull in shunting operations and shunters and enginemen took 20min for breakfast. When the footplatemen came back the fire was out! Shunters, ready to restart work, waved their lamps for the engine to come down on to a line of trucks. On being informed that there would be a slight technical delay due to the fire being out, the shunters ran round the sheds and came back with several broken wooden packing cases, which the fireman broke up with the coal pick. The wood, together with several shovelfuls of hard coal and a pint of paraffin and the contents of the oil-can were put into the firebox and within 20min the little engine was on the boil again!

The shunting yards were the training ground for firemen who learned to drive the engine under the guiding eye of their driver. The shunters were generally very patient with a fireman under tuition—especially if he was a little timid to 'hit 'em up', though they soon shouted if the fireman was

F
87

too eager. The fireman was instructed to have faith in the shunters' hand signals, which by night were: white light waved from side to side across the shunters body meant 'come ahead'. When the light was waved in double quick time 'hit 'em up', which was always followed by a red light, upon which the engine brake handle was dropped and the trucks went on by momentum. A green light held steadily indicated 'slow down'—a relic of the early days of railways when green indicated caution, and a white light moved towards and away from the engine was for 'reverse'. The shunters were adept at changing the colour of their hand lamps by a flick of the wrist and without the necessity of looking at their lamp while they did so. When the fireman was relaying the shunter's instructions to his driver, the above words were all that were spoken.

Experience in the shunting yards was invaluable to a fireman, for it was here he learned the vital differences in the operation of the vacuum and Westinghouse compressed air brakes. In dry weather, the Brighton Westinghouse-equipped engines pulled up much more quickly than a vacuum-braked engine, but in wet weather the Westinghouse had to be applied and released in bursts otherwise the engine locked her wheels and let the trucks drag her along. Approaching wagons one learned not to release the Westinghouse brake and then immediately re-apply it, since the brake cylinders did not have sufficient time to re-charge. Once the fireman had mastered the technique of stopping and starting, he was allowed to get on with shunting.

It was also on shunting duties, which sometimes had quiet periods, that the fireman gained knowledge of the rule book. Drivers would ask such questions as 'When can you start a train against the signals?' 'What does a yellow flag held by a signalman indicate?' By the light of an open firehole door many a fireman has learned the intricacies of wrong line orders and setting an engine to be right for oiling.

By the time a fireman was in No 4 link, he was beginning to have a good knowledge of the rule book and the execution of those rules. By this time, all firemen had learned how to stop a passenger train if the engine is partially derailed (by using the train release trigger on the brake valve which applied the train brakes and not the engine brakes). The value of this method was ably demonstrated when a Merchant Navy class Pacific broke a driving axle while descending Crewkerne bank at speed, the driver managed to stop the train in $\frac{3}{4}$ mile, without completely derailing the disabled engine.

At Bricklayers Arms, as at most locomotive depots, firemen had their favourite engine—one which would 'steam on a candle'. Engine No 1315, an unrebuilt class E 4-4-0, was one such engine, even though she was sometimes referred to as 'the killer' since two men had been killed by her. On the Gillingham van train, which left London Bridge, Low Level, early on a Saturday evening, 1315 would take a long train of vans down to Gillingham, with her firehole doors open all the way. On the Margate (excursions) from Blackheath or Deptford, she would clock-up a very steady 75mph with her steam-pressure hovering on the full working pressure of 180lb/sq in. Bricklayers Arms had six other E class engines— 1166, 1176, 1273, 1491, 1175 and 1275. No 1275 was one of a pair (No 1036 was the other) converted to superheating by Harry Wainwright back in 1912. No 1036 had been fitted with a Schmidt superheater while No 1275 had received a Robinson pattern. Both engines had had their working pressure reduced to 160lb/sq in, yet until bridge strengthening was completed in the middle 1930s, these two engines (then attached to Longhedge and later Stewarts Lane had double-headed some of the boat trains out of Victoria. No 1275 also had the nickname of 'Wheezy Anna' after the sound emitted from her front end when she was running at low-speed. Many had tried to diagnose the squeeky-groan she made when starting—even Ashford Works could not cure it. One day at The Brick, the driver of No 1275 decided to steam a piece of haddock for his tea. The firing shovel was duly cleaned and the haddock placed on it, underneath the injector overflow pipe. The engine was standing on the crane road, next to the wall of the Carriage Shed. The fireman turned on live steam to the injector to steam the haddock, but the strength of youth turned on the steam full-blast and the haddock ascended into the air and then slid down the greasy, grimy wall of the Carriage Shed. No 1275 was, for some time after this event, referred to as 'the flying haddock'!

Many old customs have died out as the years have gone by, and one missed by enginemen before the end of steam was that of the hop pickers' specials, generally referred to as 'oppers'. For many, many years, hop picking was the traditional holiday of many Londoners who chose to spend their fortnight's holiday (without pay in those days) earning a few pounds picking hops in the gardens of Kent. By 1947, hop picking was on the decline as holidays with pay became the general thing, but quite a few 'oppers were run in the late forties and early fifties. Coaching stock was usually the old South Eastern birdcage stock that only came out of the rusty sidings at Maze Hill or Blackheath for such trains or the Margates. Apart from the hop pickers themselves there were also the hop pickers' friends' specials. Some idea of the hopper traffic can be gained by the figures for 1947 when 50 specials were run, with 20,869 tickets issued, while over 70,000 tickets were issued for hop pickers' friends' specials.

The hop-picking fraternity started queueing at London Bridge, Low Level, around midnight, in order to be on the first trains down—any time after 4 am. Engines 1275 and 1315 were the star performers on these trains which were tightly timed. Some trains ran over the Oxted line, some to Paddock Wood ran via Maidstone West and Yalding and a few ran down the main line via Orpington. Any delays en route brought forth Cockney comments from the travellers, few of which were printable. Platelayers kept well clear of these trains since empty beer bottles were thrown from them by the merrymakers on their way down; even at six in the morning drinking was well under way.

The Margate and Ramsgate excursions were more refined,

though a few travellers were rather the worse for wear by the time the train stopped at Herne Bay. The usual load was a nine-coach birdcage set and often a D class 4–4–0 was withdrawn from store at New Cross Gate shed and made ready for the road. These trains usually left Blackheath around 7–9 am and called at Woolwich Arsenal, Dartford, Gravesend Central then fast to Whitstable. Trains from Deptford called at Greenwich, Woolwich Arsenal and Dartford. B Arms had three D class 4–4–0s—1488, 1591 and 1746. Tonbridge Shed had Nos 1549, 1496, 1728, 1729, 1730, 1731 and 1733. The engines could certainly go and could make steam readily. Older drivers used to tell the fireman to put his injector on and forget it. The 6ft 8in driving wheels took steam as fast as the boiler could produce it, but the injector was unable to maintain the water level when the engines were worked hard, particularly over the Maidstone East route, so that it was often necessary for the driver to put his injector on in order to keep a reasonable level of water in the boiler. After the summer season, the Ds usually went back into store in the Croydon shed at New Cross Loco.

While engines in steam were un-manned, they were looked after by the firelighters (later re-named steam-raisers) whose job it was to ensure that engine fires were kept made up to be ready for the road once the fireman had spread the fire all over the box; most important of all boilers were kept topped up with water from time to time. This last duty was sometimes done too well, and the firelighters used to fill the boilers right up—a bad practice since water expands and rises as temperature increases. On superheated engines moreover the practice was dangerous. One afternoon, Driver Ted Biggs and his mate had to prepare one of Tunbridge Wells's beautiful J class Pacific tanks. Immaculately cleaned No 2325 stood in the Carriage Shed and Driver Biggs set the points for his mate to bring her out of the shed for a skip of coal. The fireman turned on the Westinghouse donkey pump, opened the cylinder cocks, relased the handbrake, put the engine in forward gear, sounded the whistle and gently opened the regulator. From within there was a 'chonk' and No 2325 moved out of the shed at a very smart pace indeed; her boiler was full-up to the whistle and with water drawn in her regulator could not be closed. Standing by the slip road points was an ex-New Cross driver, Percy Garrish who shouted to Ted Biggs 'She's bolting, mate' and quickly changed the points so that the big tank did not run on to the coal road and take all the other engines waiting there down to Dunton Road Bridge. Ted tried to board her, but the 2325 was too quick for him. Past the coal road she sped, the fireman's efforts to stop her with insufficient air pressure in the brake system were to no avail, but he put her into reverse and back she came. Foreman Foote ran up the turntable road and stopped an Arthur just in time and by this time Ted Biggs had managed to board her and put the engine in neutral, opened the regulator wide and then slammed it shut. There she stood outside the Carriage Shed, with steam still wisping from her cylinder cocks—her handbrake hard on! Driver Biggs stood cursing the Brighton Railway, its engines and the like but really he should have directed his abuse at the firelighters.

The following week, Ted, in No 6 gang, had the 1.30 am goods from New Cross Gate Yard to Norwood Yard. His engine was another Brighton type, this time E4, No 2463. The load was 30 wagons of coal and the E4 was officially capable of taking that load up Forest Hill bank without a banking engine, not that one was available, anyway. Generally 2463 was the pilot engine in Willow Walk, and when Ted and his mate relieved the crew on her just before midnight they were not to know just how badly her cylinders needed repacking. All that week, B Arms had been coaling its engines with best Yorkshire hards and the little Brighton Tankie had a bunkerful of them.

Promptly at 1.30 am the guard gave a green light from his brake-van and settled down in his look-out corner to watch the signals for the 25min run to Norwood. Had he been able to foretell the future he would most likely have curled up and gone to sleep. By the time 2463 had passed under New Cross Road overbridge, the regulator was three parts open, with steam whimpering at her safety valves—how the boiler liked that hard coal. Slowly she barked her way towards Brockley —slowly was the word, for it took her 16min to reach there. As soon as steam pressure went below 150lb the train came to a stand. At 3.10 am the signalman at Forest Hill had still not sighted the goods train he had accepted at 2.35! Driver Biggs stopped at Forest Hill box at 3.20 am and was put back into the long coal sidings since the engine was almost out of water, and, more important, the Brighton paper train was not used to being held at Forest Hill! The engine later went light to Norwood Loco for water. For some time Ted Biggs was known as 'the Brighton speed king'. Upon returning to The Brick, Biggs put in a repair card for engine 2463 upon which he wrote under the column headed 'work required. Don't bother—just scrap her'. Nobody took it seriously and 2463 lingered on another 12 years.

Another class of engine—a South Eastern design—to do excellent work was the O1 class, an 0–6–0 tender goods dating back to 1878. These old Stirling engines were rebuilt between 1912 and 1916 with H class boilers, their original pressure of 140lb/sq in being increased by 10lb. The steam reversing gear was removed from inside the cab and placed vertically on the footplate so that the steam reverse cylinder was directly level with the driver's abdomen, causing the engines to be known as 'abdomen roasters' though the actual word used was not abdomen. Nevertheless, the O1s were very useful engines and B Arms had four—Nos 1044, 1064, 1395 and 1066 'Battle of Hastings'. They steamed freely on the worst coal and hauled the coal trains from Dartford, goods from Hoo and Bexleyheath; their speciality was the Plumstead pilot, where their spark-arresting chimneys gave them the sole right to enter Woolwich Arsenal. Before entering the Arsenal premises the driver and fireman had to hand to the War Department police their pipe, tobacco, matches or lighter as a fire precaution. This little ceremony never failed to amuse enginemen who invariably asked the policeman if they required the engine fire to be put out as well; to this well-worn enquiry, the WD police had a suitable well-worn answer.

Close to Plumstead Sidings was the local council's refuse disposal plant, which during those austere days, used to boil potato peelings which were collected in special bins from the public for that purpose. The strong odour of simmering peelings earned the Plumstead duty the name of 'the piggery pilot'. When all the evening shunting was done and the trains made up, the piggery pilot used to run the late night goods to Bricklayers Arms. The O1 would have behind her anything up to 45 wagons and a brake van. From Plumstead to Woolwich Dockyard the engine would hurry along on 20 per cent cut-off with the regulator fully open in the first port, but once Charlton was reached, the regulator was opened wide so as to get a good run at the climb through Blackheath tunnel. On entering the tunnel, with the lever on 45 per cent the 0–6–0 would storm up through the tunnel, with a rain of sparks shooting out of her chimney and in spite of her spark arresting gear! Firing was simple—just five shovelfuls at a time round the firebox and, with the injector on, the engine would keep pressure around the 150 mark. In the tunnel the noise and the smoke was out of all proportion to the size of the O1, since Blackheath tunnel was on the small size and the smoke tended to beat down from the tunnel roof into the cab.

One of the worries on the footplate was to have an engine that was priming. The gauge glass would fill up with bubbles and froth, making it extremely difficult to determine the level of the water. If the fireman let the engine blow off, the water would lift through the safety valves, wasting steam and water and showering sooty water out of her chimney. The danger was in getting water in the front end, which could be extremely dangerous since water is incompressible, and a bent piston could be the result. The cause of priming was the accumulation of too much scale or sediment in the boiler, either because it was overdue for a washout or the use of too much hard water. Most locomotive depots had their own soda ash treatment plants which softened the water before it was delivered to the water cranes, but in certain areas untreated water was used and although enginemen generally tried to avoid taking water at these places, sometimes circumstances made it unavoidable.

Bulleid appreciated the dangers of priming engines and in order to cut down the weekly shed days when boilers were washed out—a filthy, wet and thoroughly unpleasant job for the boilerwashers, even though they were dressed in waterproof clothing and wore wooden clogs—he had fitted the French system of blowing down engines while out on the road. This was achieved by a blow down valve under the engine which ejected boiler sediment and water. The operation was carried out at determined spots each trip and reduced shed time.

Relieving Ramsgate men at Ashford one morning, Driver Joe Simmonds—one of the most conscientious men at B Arms —and myself took over 34081 *92 Squadron*. Joe always used to blow down between Ashford and Pluckley, to be finished before we passed through the station. Once we got *92 Squadron* moving along nicely, Driver Simmonds pointed to the two wheels which operated the blow-down equipment. With the injector on and with 265lb on the clock, we commenced the operation which, by a clock which worked when blowing down was under way, indicated seven seconds, all the time that was required. At the seventh second I closed one wheel and rapidly turned the next, but it snapped off in my hand, leaving steam and water still roaring out beneath us. Bulleid had designed the spindles four-sided and with the aid of the smallest size spanner ($\frac{3}{8}$in) and two halfpennies we slowly closed the valve. By this time, however, we were almost at Pluckley station (at which we did not call). Standing on the platform edge were the morning office workers, waiting for the stopping train that followed us. Joe hung on to the whistle cord as we passed through—the ejected steam sprayed dirt and water over the waiting passengers as we sped by and then, and only then, did the valve finally close. The second injector was put on as the level in the gauge glass was very low. By the time we reached Tonbridge, an inspector was waiting for us since the many complaints from passengers at Pluckley had been telephoned ahead of us. We never heard another word about this incident, but the future operation of the blow down valve was not so popular with us.

In 1949, however, the shape of things to come was brought home to enginemen when two 0–6–0 diesel-electric shunting engines replaced the H class tanks on duties in No 3 yard and at High Level sidings. First introduced at Norwood in 1937, the DE locomotives stayed away from their depot for a week at a time. One fireman, standing in the lobby at B Arms commented 'No fire to clean on those engines'; his driver's reply gave him food for thought though: 'No fireman either!'

6

The last Governor

The opening of the 1950s saw Bricklayers Arms enter its 106th year as a motive power depot and the last decade of its life, the most eventful period of its history. The new owners British Railways, decided that each engine should show its shed allocation by a metal shed-code plate, rivetted to the smokebox door—the code for B Arms was 73B. Several New Cross men commented that this method was a very expensive way of showing an engine's home depot as back in Brighton days, engines had their allocation painted on the front buffer angle iron: New + was for New Cross, B'ton for Brighton and so on. It is interesting to note that from 1973, Southern Region electric multiple-unit stock has had its home depot, in code, under the left-hand cab window; Brighton-based stock is painted B'ton, Selhurst, S'hurst and so on. Obviously the old Brighton Railway had the right idea so many years before!

In the early part of 1950, H. Packham retired from the position of Bricklayers Arms running shed superintendent. In true style, the vacancy was advertised throughout the Southern system and while applications were received and sifted, a temporary governor was appointed to look after The Brick; his title was that of shed master. This new title, imported from a foreign region, conjured up an image of someone who was a cross between a work house master, out of a Dickens' novel and a top-hatted ring master from a circus! Certainly, some officials at Waterloo were of the opinion that to run B Arms Loco a candidate with circus experience would have a decided advantage.

The temporary shed master was Charles H. Boarer, who

97

had commenced his railway career with the South Eastern & Chatham Railway in 1918 as a fitter's apprentice at B Arms. He went on to become a fitter at Margate Shed and then to leading fitter at Gillingham Loco when Margate closed down in 1926. His previous two appointments were as foreman fitter, Stewarts Lane, thence to running shed superintendent at Tonbridge, in July 1948.

Charles Boarer found that morale at The Brick was at a low ebb when he arrived, being way down the monthly time-keeping (or losing) tables, pinned up at every depot on the Southern. Stewarts Lane and Dover were at the top of the Eastern Section and Bournemouth on the Western. B Arms was bottom but one! The tables were based on time lost by locomotive causes, per thousand train miles and were an accurate reflection on each and every depot.

A board was held at Waterloo to decide the first (and incidentally the last) shed master for Bricklayers Arms depot. Mr T. E. Chrimes was in the chair, ably assisted by Mr G. L. Nicholson, divisional motive power superintendent. Lots of questions were fired at the applicants and a short time afterwards Mr Boarer received a visit from G. L. Nicholson, who informed him that the permanent job at B Arms was his. He wished Charles Boarer good luck and added 'You will need all you can get'.

He took over in May 1950, and allocated to his care were over 120 engines: 4 King Arthurs, 18 Schools, 10 L1 4–4–0s, 4 N 2–6–0s, 6 E1 (SECR), and 7 E 4–4–0s, 4 D 4–4–0s, 16 C and 4 O1 0–6–0s, 11 H 0–4–4Ts, 2 U1 2–6–0s, 1 S 0–6–0ST, 3 I1X 4–4–2Ts, 3 B4X 4–4–0s, 2 E1 (LBSC) 0–6–0Ts, 10 E3, 8 E4, 3 E5, 5 E6, all 0–6–2Ts, 6 C2X 0–6–0s and 6 WD class 2–8–0s.

The Southern's lack of stabling points for coaching stock, forced it to resort to the practice of moving the trains about. In the morning, some of the empty trains were taken from Cannon Street, by an H 0–4–4 tank up to the closed Ludgate Hill station, where the H tank ran round its train and took the empties to Stewarts Lane. In the afternoon the coaches returned via Brockley Lane to Blackheath and then worked back to London. With a nickname for most things these duties were often called an out and up and down and back! In No 4 link there was a duty to prepare a Pacific, take empties from Rotherhithe Road to Grove Park Sidings, run round the train ready to work up to London, make up the fire and shovel coal forward in the tender, piling as many large knobs of coal on the footplate beforehand to make up the fire at the last possible minute and at the same time keep the damperless engine quiet and as smokeless as possible during the hour waiting close to a dense residential area. The fire was bare at the front of the box and was bad firing practice but the only way to keep her quiet. The Grove Park duty was often called a down, round and back turn. This duty really arose because there was nowhere to stable coaches at Charing Cross or Cannon Street, and Rotherhithe Road sidings, with their exit to the South Eastern main line from B Arms facing towards New Cross, a reversal was necessary in any case. Grove Park was the first suitable point where a locomotive could run-round. Today Grove Park has electric train berthing sidings built specially as part of the 1962 Dover main line electrification scheme.

At the end of the 1940s, and early 1950s Bricklayers Arms was very short of firemen—indeed from the end of world war two, it had never possessed a single passed cleaner. As soon as a cleaner reached the age of sixteen, he was promoted to fireman, even though he did not get his cap-badge and serge jacket immediately. The system of recruitment for footplate-men had changed little from the inception of railways: cleaner, passed cleaner, fireman, passed fireman, driver.

Until the outbreak of world war two, temporary cleaners (as opposed to permanent cleaners—men who had failed the eyesight test but preferred to remain engine cleaners) had to do 313 firing turns before they could apply for an advertised vacancy for a fireman. The vacancies were circulated to *all* depots on the Southern Railway, so that a vacancy for a fire-man was filled only by the most senior passed cleaner. It was in sheer desperation that men at Margate Shed would apply for a vacancy at Bricklayers Arms, for example, even though this involved living away from home, in order to gain promotion.

By 1949, youths of 16 were allowed to do night work, so that they were put straight into a link. The National Service Act, 1948, contributed to the shortage of firemen, since lads of 18 years and over had to do 18 months' service in the armed forces, increased to two years in October 1950, which affected links 4 and 3, which lost all firemen during the year.

Firemen returning from their period of national service were catered for by a special two-day re-habilitation course. The first part was held in the staff cinema, underneath Waterloo station, where a series of films were shown outlining a fireman's duty and the avoidance of accidents. The second part of the course was held on Chislehurst station, in the disused waiting rooms on the main line platforms. A locomotive inspector, with the aid of a model railway, showed how to protect trains in various stages of disablement, and the course ended with an oral and written examination concerning signals, rules and footplate procedure.

With constant gaps caused by calling-up trained firemen, promotion of young firemen through the links was too fast and engine performance on the road suffered through badly made-up fires before the run commenced. Shunting duties in High Level and No 3 Yards often involved banking a train up to Forest Hill, after working transfer freight to New Cross Gate Yard. One duty provided banking assistance to the 12.05 am New Cross Gate–Brighton freight, which by that time was generally hauled by one of the Southern's three electric locomotives (CC1, CC2 and CC3). The engines were always called the 'Hornbys' and to watch an E5, radial with a junior fireman doing his best, while the driver tried to give banking assistance to the train, was a sight indeed. The E5, would have to allow the brake van of the 12.05 to clear the points in front of it (the banker was generally on the adjacent road to the train to allow the pilot engine to make up the train) before it could move, then it was a dash to catch the Hornby train, let alone provide actual banking! The radial would shoot sparks all the way up Forest Hill bank and by the time Forest Hill box was reached, the fireman had had enough. Running back light to B Arms, the little Brighton tank engine would have both injectors on to get the water level in the boiler to a respectable depth.

The trials of banking goods trains were the least of the new governor's worries. The London evening papers were again slating the business trains out of Charing Cross and Cannon Street—particularly the latter, a large proportion of which were Bricklayers Arms duties. Charles Boarer had already tackled the problems of lost time by the tightening up of maintenance and repair work on engines in and out of B Arms.

The new governor would appear in the sheds, attired in overalls, and help with repair work—not just with advice either and sometimes could be seen inside fireboxes being re-stayed, checking the working time of boilersmiths. Word soon got around that the new bloke was not averse to taking his coat off. Enginemen were pleasantly surprised to find fitters waiting for their engine as it came off the turntable road. Any fitter who took an unreasonable time on a job was bawled out by Foreman Fitter Bert Wood or Charlie Richford. Firemen who were late for duty too often, suddenly found themselves on the carpet in front of the governor himself, instead of the customary good natured ticking off from chief clerk Ernest Baughen.

The newspaper criticism, however, could not go unanswered, but the public relations department's usual replies about the fitting of steam trains into the world's heaviest electric train service, were beginning to fall on deaf ears. The fact that some of the delays were the customers' own fault could not be mentioned—how many of us still look for that empty corner seat *after* the guard has whistled for all aboard? With trains timed in half minutes, a half-minute delay in starting was fateful.

The divisional motive power superintendent (G. L. Nicholson) called his shed masters to a conference, and in no uncertain terms stated that the Southern was deeply concerned that its life-blood, the season ticket holders (the word commuter had yet to cross the Atlantic) found just cause to complain of bad time-keeping by steam trains. Reliability of the engine on the road was, without question, the shed master's job, but subject to decent coal being available, engine performance was well and truly in the hands of the two men on the engine. Charles Boarer passed the DMPS's sentiments to his men at The Brick. Steam trains were frequently halted outside Borough Market Junction to let an electric train go by, and the driver then had to restart an 11 coach train on a sharp, check-railed curve, losing about $2\frac{1}{2}$min even for a brief stop there. In spite of the crews' efforts to regain lost time, the travellers de-training at such stations as Sevenoaks or Chatham were only concerned that their train was late again. On the Central Section workings, delays at East Croydon gave rise to complaints of late arrival from the residents of Oxted and East Grinstead, though these were rare compared with the Eastern Section workings.

The Traffic Department ensured that station staff gave their closest co-operation to get trains away from stations as quickly as possible, so that the ball was well and truly in the enginemen's court.

The new Shed Master at B Arms spent evening after evening on the footplate of his engines—after a full day's work in the office—to see for himself if his men were at fault. The best way to find out if engines were properly ready for the road was to walk on to Cannon Street bridge, to the siding where engines waiting to back on their trains were standing, with the No 4 link men getting the engine ready. Unannounced, Mr Boarer climbed up into the cab of a West Country. The fire was above the level of the mouthpiece, there was enough coal stacked up on the engine end of the tender to get down to the coast and back. All the trimmings were in, cab lights cleaned and everything in good order. Satisfied that one

Above: One of the last regular workings for a rebuilt SECR 4-4-0 was the morning Holborn Viaduct–Ramsgate train although in last years it started from London Bridge. It is seen speeding downhill from Sevenoaks tunnel past Weald Intermediate signalbox where it passes a Hastings–Cannon Street diesel multiple-unit in July 1960.

Derek Cross

Below: A rebuilt SECR Class D1 4-4-0 leaves Margate with a summer special up via Chatham and Nunhead.

Rev A. C. Cawston

Contrasting main line duties of the type performed by Bricklayers Arms crews: *above*, Battle of Britain Pacific No 34050 *Royal Observer Corps* accelerates through Paddock Wood with the 9.10 Charing Cross–Ramsgate on 6 May 1961 in the last weeks of steam working in Kent.

D. T. Cobbe

Below: Some Bricklayers Arms turns included the working of through portions from North of England–South Coast trains, some of which divided at Redhill. Here B Arms LMS type 2-6-4T No 42081 leaves Redhill with the Hastings portion of the through train from Birkenhead on 10 July 1954.

Stanley Creer

engine was all right was not enough for the governor, who visited two more and then walked back to the station.

One of the main sources of complaint, was the poor time-keeping of the 6.18 from Cannon Street to Deal, a No 2 link duty, so for his first ride down, Charles Boarer climbed up into the cab of Schools class No 30935 *Sevenoaks* and told the crew to forget he was there. It was a Friday night, and the load was 11 coaches, 390 tons gross (Mondays to Thursdays the load was only 10). Promptly at 6.16 pm, the Ramsgate via Chislehurst Junction, left the adjacent platform, and was booked to run through No 2 road at London Bridge and continue on the local line to Chislehurst Junction where she veered left towards Chatham. With a lower speed limit through London Bridge and the fact that the train was almost always checked at Borough Market Junction, the 6.16 and the 6.18 generally ran side by side all the way to Chislehurst station. Passengers in the trains used to bet with each other as to which train would get its engine to the London end of Chislehurst platform first. Inducement to enginemen was not unknown, but with or without bets, the Ramsgate crew on the 6.16 and the Bricklayers Arms crew on the 6.18, regarded these duties as a point of honour to be first, for the sake of their depot, and called the duties the race trains or sometimes the mad quarter of an hour, though in fact 16min were allowed. Ramsgate generally provided a spam, though an Arthur or Schools sometimes put in an appearance. Brick-layers Arms hardly ever varied from a Schools on the 6.18.

So it was that with rude whistling from the Ramsgate spam, the 6.16 pulled out of Cannon Street, only to be brought to a dead stand outside Borough Market. At 6.17½, the station foreman gave a yellow flag to the B Arms crew, since with eleven coaches on, the Schools was past the starting signal. At 6.18, the guard gave the right away, and with sand on, No 30935 pulled out. The 6.16 was still waiting . . . but the 6.18 was also stopped. Charles Boarer made notes. As the clock on Southwark Cathedral pointed to 6.21, the aspect changed to two yellows and the 6.16 moved off, with violent slipping, soon brought under control. At 6.21$\frac{1}{2}$, the 6.18 got a green and with just a suspicion of a slip *Sevenoaks* pulled her train steadily round the curve. The fireman, leaning well out his side shouted 'green down three' and then fired the first of seven shovelfuls into the huge fire. Regulator fully open in the first port and with the reverser bridle wheel on 40 per cent the 6.18 thundered through London Bridge station, drowning the station announcer's exhortation to 'stand well back on platform three'. Even the travel-hardened businessmen looked up from their evening papers as the two steam trains, in quick succession, passed through.

With the pressure on 220 and the injector on, the driver pulled the bridle wheel back to 30 per cent; just ahead by Peak Freans a thick pall of smoke covered half of the 6.16. Green lights beckoned on the 6.18 and *Sevenoaks*, a small chimney Schools, was picking up speed nicely. A red light on the adjacent road showed that the 6.16 was only one clear section ahead. North Kent East, another seven shovelfuls and the engine takes the gentle right-hand curve outside New Cross at about 50mph. Half of New Cross station is covered by a dense blanket of spam smoke. Mr Boarer shouts to the driver 'He hasn't got his fire right, yet'. The fireman shuts the firehole doors tightly and puts the blower on just a fraction to avoid the risk of a blow-back when passing under New Cross Road bridge and through the 87yd Tanners Hill tunnel. In the cutting again, the fireman opens the firehole doors the usual one and a half inches and leans out to see the St John's starter, signal L18. His open palm indicates to his driver a green and the fireman resumes firing when the engine has rounded the St John's curve. The long climb to the summit just beyond Knockholt station has begun. The boiler is full and the injector is briefly shut-off. The driver glances at the pressure gauge—215—and gives the regulator a cuff to open it a little more, but the needle touches 220 and the fireman quickly puts on the injector to avoid wasting steam by allowing *Sevenoaks* to blow-off. The 6.18 passes Hither Green Loco, colour-light signals have given way to semaphores, and No 30935 is running beautifully. By Grove Park, the last coach of the 6.16 is clearly visible, swinging from side to side as last coaches always do.

The driver moves the reversing wheel slightly forward and the Schools responds immediately. The fireman tests the gauge glass and fires again. The safety valves are whimpering and the driver opens the regulator almost fully into the second valve, and brings the reverser back to 25 per cent. The Schools has got the bit between its teeth now and slowly begins to overhaul the 6.16. The white feather is still at the Schools' safety valve and shows that her boiler can beat the demands of her three cylinders and the injector. At Elmstead Woods, the cut-off is forward to 30 per cent with the regulator now fully open in the first port only; the 6.18 passes one, then two, then three coaches of the Ramsgate train. The fireman of the spam leans out to get a breath of cool fresh air and on looking back sees the rival rapidly overhauling him. By now passengers on the two trains are exchanging gestures— not all of them friendly—and the Ramsgate driver lengthens the cut-off of his engine, but with that typical lightning response of the Bulleid reverser, the lever flies into full forward gear and the spam protests by sending a great column of smoke skyward and slips badly to show her displeasure. The 6.18 passes the engine of the 6.16, with the B Arms men standing with their caps off as a mark of respect to a 'funeral train' (ie a train slower than oneself). Loud whistles from the Schools echoed by a double-insult reply from the spam's hooter. In spite of the keen running, the guard of the 6.18 enters in his journal passing Chislehurst, '$1\frac{1}{2}$min down'. Leaving the 6.16 behind, the driver turns to the governor and shouts 'I reckon we deserve a drop of tea' and pours out a cupful and all three take a sip!

Most B Arms men could not remember the last time a governor had ridden with them on the footplate and his personal interest in them and their problems were much appreciated. So much for the 6.18; the main problem seemed to be in the delays caused by the bottleneck at Borough

Market Junction and not through lack of effort on the part of the enginemen.

During the early part of 1951 Bricklayers Arms was given the honour of looking after the locomotive *William Shakespeare,* one of the new class 7 Britannia 4–6–2s of British Railways standard design, on view at the Festival of Britain exhibition until it closed in the late autumn. Enthusiastic cleaning gangs worked on 'Old Bill' to keep it in an excellent condition. When the Festival closed the engine went to Stewarts Lane to run the Golden Arrow. When Stewarts Lane had a new governor in 1952 R. H. N. Hardy, he even arranged for its flags to be washed at frequent intervals, so keen was he and the depot to keep *William Shakespeare* in immaculate condition.

Before the Festival closed, a 108-year-old French engine *Buddicom* was steamed at B Arms for the benefit of the press. Several firemen asked their drivers if they had found it easy to fire to her!

The Nos 1, 2, 3 and 4 links had a variety of ex-New Cross duties in their rosters and the older drivers scornfully referred to them as 'firemans day out' turns, since many of the trains had only six bird-cage coaches to haul. The duties varied from the Lillie Bridge train from New Cross Gate, which for years had the same Guard, named Gent, so that the train became known as 'Genties train' to the 3.23 am London Bridge to Brighton paper train. Another duty was the 5.08 am London Bridge to Brighton via Horsham, first stop Peckham Rye then practically all stations to Brighton, taking just $3\frac{1}{4}$ hours—a lovely ride round. Yet another ex-New Cross duty was the 8.36 am London Bridge to Brighton via East Grinstead, which had been, for many years, an I3 duty.

On the morning of 9 September 1951, the 8.36 was hauled by I3 class No 32021, a Tunbridge Wells engine, with Driver Len Johnson and Fireman Bowden on the footplate. At about 10 am, as the train was approaching East Grinstead, a serious fracture occurred in the main steam pipe and the greater part of the contents of the firebox and smokebox were ejected backwards through the firehole door, which was of the typical Brighton tip-flap pattern, into the cab. The train at once began to lose speed and would soon come to a standstill. One need not have much imagination as to the fiery condition in the cab.

Fireman Bowden was about to leave the footplate by the door on his side, when to his alarm, he saw through the fire-swept cab that Driver Johnson was in a badly dazed state, but still trying to close the regulator and in grave danger of being burned to death. Without hesitation, Fireman Bowden crossed the footplate to aid his driver and in so doing exposed himself to the full force of the discharging fire. He dragged Driver Johnson from the engine and without a doubt saved his life. From the serious burns he received, Bowden was rushed to the Queen Victoria Hospital in East Grinstead, where so many burned servicemen were treated during the war. Fireman Bowden spent a considerable time in that hospital.

On 27 February 1952 Her Majesty Queen Elizabeth at Buckingham Palace, presented Fireman Bowden, with the George Medal, the award of which her father King George VI had approved just two days before he died. Because of the injuries he sustained Bowden was unable to resume his career on the footplate and became a clerk in B Arms time office. Driver Johnson recovered and continued driving.

Another unfortunate incident occurred in 1951. In the previous chapter we met Driver Joe Simmonds—a very conscientious driver, indeed. Each disposal or preparation carried out by Joe was meticulous to a degree. Joe always carried a spare pair of overalls with him, tied with a belt, worn for oiling up. The regular set were worn only for driving. Driver Simmonds took an E1 rebuilt coppertop up to Rotherhithe Road, and stood at the signals there. About twelve hours earlier, a K class ex-Brighton 2-6-0, No 32347, had been lit-up after being stopped for repairs. As students of Southern locomotives will know, a vital difference between Brighton and other Southern locomotives is the fact that Brighton regulators opened in the opposite direction to other engines. One was said to pull down on a Brighton regulator to start whereas one pulled up on South Eastern engines. The men who lit-up No 32347 were unaware of this difference as the engine's regulator was left (or moved by someone else) in the open position. Five minutes after Driver Simmonds had left B Arms Loco, the crewless Mogul had enough steam to leave the yard, since its handbrake was off and reversing lever not left in mid-gear. Foreman Foote tried to board the Mogul, but she was moving much too quickly for him. With a clear road ahead, the Mogul eventually hit the E1 at a speed of about 20mph and Driver Simmonds was catapulted across the footplate and severely injured.

7

Teddy Bears, time and motion, and tradition

Early in 1952 the South Eastern Section received the first of the smaller British Railways standard locomotives. To be exact the engines were to run over the Central Section, to replace the former LBSC engines which were gradually being withdrawn, but since Stewarts Lane and B Arms covered many of these duties, together with the old Brighton shed at Tunbridge Wells, it is fair to say that the first small 2–6–2Ts were shedded at a South Eastern depot.

British Railways produced three types of tank locomotive —a light 2–6–2T of class 2, a larger 2–6–4T of class 4, the Fairburn London, Midland & Scottish design (not unnaturally called the 'Midlands'), and a similar size 2–6–4 tank engine, the BR version of another basically LMS design, some of which were built at Brighton Works and because they were numbered in the 80000 series, were called the eighty-thousands. We generally knew the small 2–6–2Ts as 'teddy bears' but 'Mickey Mouse' was sometimes used elsewhere.

Gradually the standard classes pushed out the I3 4–4–2Ts and H1 and H2 Atlantics on the Oxted, East Grinstead and Horsted Keynes duties. The problem turn on Central Section duties covered by Bricklayers Arms was the 4.20 pm from London Bridge to Brighton via Oxted. With an I3, the B Arms men found it difficult to pass Forest Hill in 9min and faired little better when an Atlantic was sustituted. With the arrival of the new standard engines, things improved, though the 4.20 never had less than nine coaches on—and not the old birdcage stock which weighed about 26 tons apiece but the heavier Maunsell corridor stock taring 30 tons or so each.

Just as Stewarts Lane, with the terrible 6.10 pm from Victoria
to Uckfield, had found it hard to pass Balham in 9min, so
the B Arms men thundered up Forest Hill bank, that splendid
2½ miles of 1 in 100, with one of the new Midland class 4
tanks. One would have to thrash a Midland all the way to
Sydenham. After the East Croydon stop, it was uphill all
the way to the next stop at Oxted. The injectors on the LMS
2–6–4Ts were not all that they might have been, and No 2
link had some anxious moments on the 4.20. The run was
all the more exciting when the 4.22 electric from London
Bridge to Tattenham Corner would try to overhaul the 4.20,
resulting in a steam versus electric contest from Honor Oak
Park as far as Anerley.

Soon the 80000 class 2–6–4Ts were diagrammed to work
the 4.20. They were big, impressive engines, but in spite
of their higher working pressure, 225lb compared with the
200lb of the LMS 2–6–4Ts and the teddy bears did not seem
to have the guts for hard uphill work. These engines were
fitted with speedometers, and every fireman would take the
opportunity of standing in front of it and ask the driver to
estimate his speed. The driver's estimate was never more
than 2 or 3mph out, and their long years of experience had
made superfluous the addition of a speedometer.

The 80000s had a three-colour gauge which indicated
if oil was being fed to the cylinders. The regulator had to be
left slightly open when making a stop, the needle on the
gauge moving from a green shaded section to a yellow section.
If the regulator was closed the needle entered a red section.
It was rumoured that a fireman, noticing the needle on red
shouted to his mate this information, amidst the clatter on
the footplate the driver only heard one word 'red' and
immediately dropped the brake handle! The reversing wheel
was set edge-on to the bridle rod and after some time the
nickname '80000' was dropped in favour of the 'bacon slicers',
because the likeness of the reversing wheel to that once
familiar item in every provision shop.

Now and again, a teddy bear would be put on the 4.20 and

although steam would drop to 170lb going up Forest Hill bank, once over the top it would come round quickly. They were really grand little engines and both B Arms and Tunbridge Wells men loved them. You could make the fire up, close the damper and they would stand quietly, as good as gold. Five minutes before starting time, open the damper, a touch on the blower and round they would come. No 2 link did quite a bit of running around over the Oxted and Bluebell lines. Once the South Eastern men had learned the road, they thoroughly enjoyed the friendly atmosphere of the little stations south of East Grinstead—many of which are sadly no more. Happily a five-mile slice between Sheffield Park and Horsted Keynes remains in operation, by steam, to remind us all what it was like.

After relief in Brighton station on arrival at 6.46, the return leg, of the 4.20 pm down, was passenger to Lewes and relieve on the 7.46 pm from Brighton, after a meal break. At 8.19 pm the crew left for London Bridge via Sheffield Park, spending 5min at East Grinstead—from 9.08 to 9.13 and finishing with a very fast sprint from East Croydon to London Bridge, arriving at 10.17 pm. That last lap was literally galloped, and it was not unusual to pass Forest Hill at 60mph and touch 75mph between Honor Oak Park and Brockley, before checking for the 65mph limit through New Cross Gate.

Instead of the usual teddy bear on this duty, Driver Tom Merrett (a former New Cross driver) and his mate relieved one evening at Lewes on an E5 radial 0-6-2T, No 32590. The fireman shook his head and said something to the effect that they were going to get a ticket (lost time) with 'that fugitive from the shunting yard'. Tom replied that when he was in the top link at New Cross, he had fired radials on main line turns and that they could really go. Tom handled that radial as if she was still a top link engine and in spite of a bunkerful of Brighton's best briquettes, they kept time. Their descent of Forest Hill bank, was, in the words of the fireman 'unbelievable' and their arrival at London Bridge at 10.17 proof of the driver's faith and skill.

In the summer of 1952, the 'razor gang'—or to give them their official title the time and motion study—men cast their eyes on B Arms, whose reputation for long hours was well known. One bright day, a T&M man went down to the accounts office at Ashford, to trace 24 hours in the life of a B Arms Schools. By assembling all the relevant drivers' tickets for this particular engine, he was astounded to learn some impossible feats. According to one ticket, the Schools was being prepared by Driver X and Fireman Y, yet, according to another, the self same engine, at the time stated by Driver X, was somewhere between Grove Park and Orpington en route to Dover with Driver A and Fireman B!

The telephone in Mr Boarer's office was soon echoing with a call from T&M. The voice on the phone informed the B Arms' governor of flagrant, wilful misrepresentation of time and facts on a driver's waybill. CB listened and said he knew of them and had signed the relevant tickets. A long silence ensued and after a while Mr Boarer asked if the voice was still there. The voice said that T&M would be paying a three-day visit to Bricklayers Arms and that Mr Boarer would hear more about this. Moreover after the visit was concluded the overtime which was situation normal at Bricklayers Arms would be cut by half and incorrect entries on drivers' tickets would be completely eliminated. It looked as though T&M were going to perform a miracle, in three days!

The T&M team duly arrived and the governor invited them to roam around and ask as many questions as they wanted. Mr Boarer requested them to observe most carefully the time engines arrived in the depot (which commenced on the city side of Dunton Road bridge) and the actual time the engines were coaled. As was usual any morning from Monday to Friday, the long line of engines extended well past Dunton Road bridge, at the country end. One T&M man told a fireman not to throw clinker out before he got to the proper place—the disposal area in the sheds. The fireman promptly complied with this request and replaced the fire-irons on the tender, where they were later buried in coal and had to be dug out.

The fireman dutifully informed his driver that he was risking his safety by oiling up the engine adjacent to the out road, so that the driver came back on to the footplate.

One hour later, some choice words came from Foreman Molyneaux, who wanted to know why, this crew, with the only N class 2–6–0 in the depot, was not ready to set off for Sorting Sidings for No 123 duty, due away at 10.00 am. Molyneaux ranted on that he had seen the engine come under Dunton Road bridge at 9.00 am, yet no fire had been cleaned and although the N was coaled by 9.35 she still had not been put away and got ready (two hours' work) as she normally was, so that C class 0–6–0 had to take over this duty.

Chaos reigned in the yard—no fires being cleaned on the coal road so that every engine was having its fire cleaned over the pits, instead of a quick rake-out of the ash pan and smoke-box and straight through the Old Shed to be ready for away again.

At noon, the chairman of the T&M team entered Charles Boarer's small, smoky office. The governor looked up from his desk and enquired 'ready for a quick lunch?' 'No' came the curt reply, 'We are leaving you Mr Boarer'. 'Quick three days, wasn't it?' was the Shed Master's reply. The T&M man looked at the governor 'We cannot do anything at *this* depot, Mr Boarer, since half your engines do not get into the depot until they are almost due out again—good morning—and good bye'. They never returned and the overtime and in-correct entries continued, as they had always done.

Before the reader throws up his hands in horror and trots out the old cliché that 'no wonder the railways did not pay', a look at the facts before the figures puts the whole situation, as it was then, into perspective. Steam was strictly a back-number, for electric services had priority at all times—except for royalty. Ever since the days of Sir Herbert Walker, steam had to be fitted in between the ever increasing number of electric trains, and little track occupation was available for light engine running. The previous chapter outlined how the motive power depot and traffic department had to resort to move empty coaching stock about because of the lack of suitable stabling points, train engines often being used for this purpose. By the time they got a path into the depot much of the allocated time for preparation and disposal had been eaten up. In the mornings, relief crews could be seen oiling up in Cannon Street or Charing Cross, turning the fire over so as to be ready the moment the engine got into Ewer Street for the clinker to be thrown out and the fire made up again. The St Leonards Schools had a very short time in Ewer Street before they were out again to make room for a West Country, which generally needed four or five skips of coal and very often had to go round the Borough Market Junction Spur, in order to turn, since the turntable at Ewer Street was only 49ft long, too short for a Pacific. The engine then came out of Cannon Street, into London Bridge and then tender first back to Charing Cross. All this took time and the tender had to be filled with 2,500 gallons of water, the fire made up, motion inspected and while running back to Charing Cross, the fireman gave the cab lights a clean. Whether the preparation and disposal (P&D) was carried out in Ewer Street or back at Bricklayers Arms, the men were expected, indeed they were relied upon to do two hours' work in less than one, since the engine simply could not get into the depot any earlier. Enginemen were held fully responsible for all P&D work being properly carried out no matter how short of time they were. If the layout of Bricklayers Arms depot could have been improved no money would have been available to carry it out with potential main line electrification in view.

Bricklayers Arms had a couple of sets of shed enginemen, men who could not drive on the main line because of failure to pass the eyesight test. One of the pair was Driver Bob Sweeting and his Fireman, Basil Saunders. Bob's eyesight had put him in the yard soon after he had passed for driver, though he was about ten years younger than his fireman! Bas had gone up to pass for driver and although he knew the answers he was unable to set them down on paper; rather than condemn him to a non-footplate grade, he was allowed to remain as a fireman on yard duties only. The shed enginemen were given regular turns of duty and had a set number of engines to dispose of and prepare—and a fine art they made of it. Any engine made ready by 'Bas and Bob' was an engine to be recommended.

In the early 1950s cases of hooliganism occurred in the usually respectable area of Petts Wood. The target was the 7.34 pm from Charing Cross, which had stones dropped on to the engine as it passed under a footbridge. By the time the train had made its first stop at Sevenoaks and a complaint made, the culprits had fled long before the police eventually arrived at the footbridge. One evening a stone narrowly missed Driver Bill Snell, but he did not report the matter at Sevenoaks. The following evening, however, he told his fireman to change places with him as they passed Elmstead Woods. Bill piled several shovelfuls of slack coal under the door and told the fireman to shut the regulator when he gave the word. As the 7.34 approached the footbridge, the hooligans could be seen, perched ready to bomb the engine. Bill shut off the injector with the needle just on 220, the firehole doors were shut tight and the blower only on a touch; a few yards from the bridge Bill yelled 'now', with the regulator closed suddenly, thick, black smoke rolled out of the chimney and enveloped the boys aloft and with her injector off, steam roared from the engine's safety valves as the engine passed under the bridge. No more incidents occurred for Bill that week as he reckoned that 220lb of steam and lungfuls of smoke with a slight scalding was better than a talk from a policeman any day!

As at all locomotive depots, traditions were respected. Drivers had handed them down to their firemen, who in later years passed them on to the next generation of firemen and so on. When a driver spoke of a good fireman, he referred to one who could not only give him all the steam he wanted but also to one who arrived a little before him, drew the necessary oil from the stores—and in some cases even did the oiling-up as well. He was one who always checked the tender for water, washed the footplate down and generally did all that a fireman should—and just a little more, without asking.

One tradition that both driver and fireman insisted on was that of handing over an engine in the condition that one would like to find it in. The hand-over crew who were relieved by the engine crew for the journey down were expected to have done a good job of preparation: lubricator set, trimmings in, fire made right up, plenty of coal suitably broken up shovelled forward on the tender, gauge glasses cleaned as well as the cab lights. As mentioned previously, preparing an engine at one of the London terminal stations —particularly the damperless Bulleid Pacifics—was an art in itself. At Charing Cross, smoke abatement officers ('smoke jacks') used to watch for too dense an emission of smoke, but even so, all engines were given a good start. All South Eastern men used to consider it vital to have a firebox full of fire to start. It was the same with the Brighton men, many of whom never reckoned to fire an Atlantic between London and Brighton. Much has been written about the merits of carrying a thin fire as opposed to a thick fire, but the type of coal used really dictated to a large extent the type of fire carried. No less a person than William Stroudley, laid down that a large fire should be made up, to complete firing well before the end of a run, thereby burning the fire away to be ready for cleaning, and getting the most economical use of the coal burned.

At the risk of over emphasising the difficulty in keeping the Bulleid Pacifics quiet in London, all sorts of methods were used by enginemen—leaving the regulator slightly open, with the reverse lever in neutral and the cylinder cocks open, keeping the steam dynamo on, which provided electricity for the engine headlights, injector inspection and motion illumination, and opening the steam heating cock at the front of the engine; all used steam while the engine was standing still.

Drivers impressed upon their firemen that they should

prepare the engine as if they themselves were working the train down to the coast. Sometimes, the relief fireman did not arrive and then came the moment of truth for the lower link fireman. In most cases, with expert help from the driver, the younger hands managed, but shortage of steam at the beginning of the run would most surely be attributed to a poorly made-up fire. Most of the lower link fireman used to hope that their relief would not arrive so that they could show the driver how they could manage.

Having said what was expected from a hand-over crew, we must go back to Easter 1952. At holiday times, it was customary for the Southern to run leave trains for soldiers, particularly for the many national servicemen with the armed forces. The large army camps at Shorncliffe and Dover were well catered for and after the Easter leave, a special was booked to leave London Bridge (High Level) and run fast to Ashford. It befell that two men from No 2 link were assigned this job, the fireman having just completed two years in the army. It was the practice at Stewarts Lane and Dover for firemen returning to railway service to have a running trip on a boat train, as third man, to get them into the swing of the job. B Arms, however, decided that the best way to get back to firing was to do it—not just watch, and so it was that Driver Collins was given this particular mate. Collins told his mate that the list clerk had felt sorry for an ex-soldier and had given him a 'fireman's holiday' turn (work down, home as passenger). The pair signed on at 4.30 am and walked up to London Bridge Station. They waited at the country end of platform 3, and at 5.05, in came the train, nine Maunsell coaches and a Ramsgate spam, 34082 *615 Squadron*. The relief crew climbed aboard to relieve a pair of B Arms men, who said they had prepared her at 2 am and they had been standing at Cannon Street for an hour. The fireman glanced at the pressure gauge: 220lb (working pressure 280), there was half a glass of water and the blower was on hard. The hand-over crew left the engine in a bit of a hurry. Driver Collins remained on the fireman's side to wait for the guards right away, while his mate had a look at the fire, which brought forth a long string of oaths from the fireman. In the firebox was about $\frac{1}{2}$ ton of fire, spread miserably about the firebox; no wonder the blower was hard on, since the fire was not properly alight all over. Worse was to come for the tender shovel plate was empty, due no doubt, to a blockage caused by a large knob of coal. The fireman carefully opened the tender doors, expecting a deluge of coal on to the footplate, but although there was plenty of coal on the tender, it had not been thrown forward.

The guard blew his whistle and green colour lights beckoned the train to start. Percy Collins opened the regulator and touched the whistle cord, but jokingly, upon seeing the state of the fire decided not to waste steam by sounding the whistle! The fireman shook the fire by operating the rocking grate, then shut the firehole doors while he climbed into the tender to bring down some coal. Driver Collins handled the engine gently, yet by North Kent East, pressure had fallen to 200. Injector on, and passing St Johns, at the foot of the 16 mile climb to Knockholt summit, pressure was back to 180. Firing quickly, using the steam operating doors, the fireman gradually started to build some sort of fire. Milepost $6\frac{1}{2}$, with a 1 in 140 gradient up through Hither Green which steepened to 1 in 120 at Elmstead Woods, brought no respite for the boiler, which had only 170lb on passing Orpington. The regulator was almost closed on the 1 in 310 but the needle quivered on 160. With smoke belching from her chimney the spam passed through Chelsfield, where a shake up by the rocking grate helped the fire to brighten up. Still climbing approaching Knockholt, the train was doing about 30mph, but the injector was on and the pressure had risen to 175. Over the summit—both injectors on and the very welcome help of the downhill $3\frac{3}{4}$ miles at 1 in 145 enabled them to pick up speed to emerge from Polhill tunnel at 65mph. The impetus gained swept them up the 1 in 160 climb into Sevenoaks, where at the mouth of Sevenoaks tunnel the line drops sharply down at 1 in 144 for two miles, steepening to 1 in 122 for a further four miles. All the way downhill, the fireman was building the pyramid-shaped fire that the spams loved, with just five shovelfuls at a time. During the 80mph descent in Sevenoaks tunnel, the fireman climbed into the tender to comb down more coal—a draughty and dangerous exercise. This exploit was rewarded by finding plenty of large lumps of Yorkshire hard coal, which were piled under the firehole door and into the back corners. At milepost 28½ Driver Collins shut the regulator for the approaching Tonbridge curve. For the first time on the journey, the boiler was full, and the steam pressure gauge registered 220lb. A blast on the hooter and 34082 put on steam for Ashford. According to the reverser scale, the cut-off was at 25 per cent and the fire looked quite reasonable, but there was no doubt in the enginemen's minds that the fire had not been cleaned, for by Paddock Wood, pressure had fallen to 190, yet how she flew along; reaching 75 passing Staplehurst, rising to 85 at Pluckley, even though the boiler pressure was down to 165. Her steam chest pressure was indicating 60lb of steam, paying fine tribute to the beautifully-designed steam passages of the engine.

The train arrived at Ashford on the dot in spite of the poor condition of the fire. The engine crew had worked in close harmony and nursed her along. With a proper start to a run, a spam generally used to eat the timetable. The ability of a steam locomotive, with the boiler pressure well below its normal level, to pull something out of the hat was, of course, nothing new for the old Brighton men with their class I1 and I2, had run fast trains with little above 80lb of steam, but with the heavier and more tightly timed trains of the 1950s, only the spams seemed to be able to do it. On the credit side of the I1 and I2, they certainly did not burn 45 to 55lb of coal a mile!

A short while after this trip on 34082, the fireman was put into No 2 link, and on checking the roster sheet, noticed that the same pair of men who had handed over at London Bridge on the troop train, were booked to relieve him on a Schools at London Bridge that morning. Normally it was the custom on up trains to cease firing at Knockholt so that the fire was run nicely down ready for cleaning on arrival in London. The lubricator was turned off passing Hither Green to be cool enough to drain and refill without the risk of scalding. The run up was uneventful and the driver was pleased with his new mate. Passing Orpington, where the four track area becomes rather busy, the driver kept his head well out of the cab though his ears detected the ring of the firing shovel on the shovel plate as they passed Petts Wood and again at Elmstead Woods. The driver yelled across 'it's downhill all the way to London', but the fireman fired twice more. The engine blew off passing Hither Green and again through St John's and by the time London Bridge was reached the engine was blowing her head off. The relief crew climbed aboard and looked aghast at the fire, glowing orange-red just beneath the top of the mouth piece of the firebox. The Schools ceased blowing off just long enough for the No 2 link fireman to remark to the relief crew 'You obviously thought you had done a really good job of preparation on that spam just after Easter—well that (pointing to the fire) is how it should look—good morning to you both.' The Ramsgate crew returning home that night with the engine had to go to the stores and draw a new long scoop and a short scoop in exchange for the two on board which were twisted and bent out of usable shape as if someone had tried to clean a fully made up fire!

Driver Tom Merrett had the Saturday evening 6.15 pm out of Charing Cross down to Dover on a very rainy and stormy night in the winter of 1952. His engine was 34086, and what a beauty she was. The headcode route indication was given by the electrically-lit lamps. All went well until they left Sevenoaks, where dropping down the 1 in 144 towards Hildenborough they entered Sevenoaks tunnel. Both home and distant were clear and the train rapidly picked up speed down the falling gradient. Halfway through the tunnel, Tom and his mate observed a repeater signal for one just beyond the tunnel end showing green. At about 6omph they emerged from the tunnel and were amazed to see Weald home signal at Danger. Tom dropped the handle and put 34086 into reverse, with sand on. In the pouring rain, the engine ran by the signal. The fireman went to the signalbox to see what had caused the signalman to throw the signals back to danger in their faces. The signalman pointed out that 34086 was running without headlights, since unknown to the crew, both bulbs had burned out, en route. The fireman reminded the signalman that they were booked to stop at Tonbridge, where attention could have been drawn to the irregularity without the need for stopping the train. The signalman said that they might kill a platelayer. How a platelayer could have seen to work on a pitch black night, in pouring rain, was not the concern of the watchful signalman. Tom was awarded a reprimand for running a train without proper respect for the prevailing weather conditions! The previous evening, when running the 6.18 pm out of Cannon Street, under similar weather conditions, Tom had lost 1½min—and was given a lost time ticket to prove it! This little incident made Bricklayers Arms men 'lamp happy' and for some time afterwards a spam manned or prepared by B Arms men could be easily identified by the duplicated headcode exhibited by means of both electric and paraffin lamps.

With every respect that enginemen have always had for platelayers, it was fair to say that on such a night, work on the track would have been quite impossible to carry out. Nevertheless, Driver Merrett, was subsequently awarded one day off, without pay, for running too fast under adverse weather conditions! On occasions whatever you did, you were wrong.

Before 1952 ended, the slow but sure move to oust steam became more and more apparent. For some time, men in No 2 link had suffered the indignity of spending time in the yard, as required, when the diesel from Norwood managed to run the 5.08 am via Horsham, thereby obviating the need for a steam locomotive. The indignity was made worse by the fact that Norwood depot had taken away a Bricklayers

Arms duty. Many times the diesel failed and the men from Old Kent Road and their steam locomotive were required, but as time, and diesel experience, progressed, No 2 link lost the duty. Soon after, the first men at The Brick, signed for diesel training.

After the previously mentioned incident of Merchant Navy class No 35020 *Bibby Line* breaking her driving axle while descending Crewkerne Bank, all Merchant Navy, West Country and Battle of Britain class Pacifics were withdrawn from service for checking, leaving a desperate motive power situation. King Arthurs were at once drafted in place of spams, while the redoubtable Schools deputised on many heavy expresses. Stewarts Lane, which had about 19 WC and BOB Pacifics and four Merchant Navy Pacifics was the hardest hit depot on the Eastern Section and a call for help went out. The Eastern Region lent Stewarts Lane some B1 4–6–0s, which, although better than nothing, were no substitute for the Bulleid Pacifics. How out of place these engines appeared at the head of the green trains of the Southern. The Stewarts Lane governor, Richard Hardy, a 'foreigner' himself no less, from the Eastern Region, gave his fitters and enginemen valuable help and advice so that the best possible use was made from the gift horses. As any Stewarts Lane man who was there at the time will tell you, when all the Pacifics had been checked, the B1s were sent back to their home depots in a far better condition than when they arrived. Much of the checking of the suspect axles was done at Bricklayers Arms shops, which had ultra-sonic testing equipment. It was a great relief to discover that of the 129 engines checked (110 West Country/Battle of Britain and 19 Merchant Navy engines) there were no further cases of a flawed axle.

By the end of 1952, Bricklayers Arms had moved slightly up the timekeeping table. Many ex-Brighton engines were withdrawn and the new standard classes took over from them. If enginemen thought that their troubles would be fewer now that the Brighton relics had departed, they were in for a big shock.

8

Troubles and a disaster

For many years, a day's work for a main line crew was always reckoned to be 140 miles. For every 10 miles in excess of this figure an extra hour's pay was credited, the extra payment being known as 'mileage'. Before the outbreak of world war two, The Brick had had its fair share of mileage turns; London to Dover and back, for example was 156 miles, so that $1\frac{1}{2}$ hours mileage payment per day, made pay day something to look forward to. Then there were the 'rounder' trains —Charing Cross to Ramsgate via Dover then back up to Victoria—a total trip of 180 miles. These mileage turns were of course allocated to the senior link, and considering that the driver was unlikely to be under 50 years of age, with about 35 years' service behind him, and his fireman only 20 years less, it was fair comment to say that the No 1 link earned their keep, and their mileage money. Drivers in their fifth year earned the same basic pay as a driver with 30 years of seniority, so that in today's parlance the mileage money could be termed as a proficiency payment.

After the war, time and motion studies began to seek ways of reducing running costs and mileage turns. B Arms had a top link duty where the men were relieved at Folkestone Central ($69\frac{1}{2}$ miles from Charing Cross), ate their sandwiches in the train while travelling passenger in it to Dover, on arrival at Dover shed, they prepared their engine, were relieved by Dover men in Dover station, the Dover men worked the train as far as Folkestone Central, where the B Arms men emerged from the train and worked it back to London Bridge, where they were relieved, This gave a total distance in which they worked the train of $137\frac{3}{4}$ miles. Such cutting-up of the duties saved the pennies, but gave the men in the top link no satisfaction in their job, since men in the shunting yards were pounds better off in overtime—with little of the arduous duties connected with running commuter trains, and the frustration of trying to keep time between the priority electric trains.

The rumblings in the top link were not confined to Bricklayers Arms depot, either. Men all over the system had the same grumble that they had taken maybe 40 years to reach the peak of their career—and responsibility, for far less money than a bottom link preparation and disposal fireman was getting. Most B Arms duties were to Ashford ($56\frac{3}{4}$ miles) and back so that there was not a hope of any mileage payments.

The divisional motive power superintendent (DMPS), Eastern Section, Mr G. L. Nicholson called a meeting at which all the Shed Masters concerned attended. The venue chosen was appropriate to the subject of the meeting. The subject: Rounder Trains; the place: Folkestone, where so many duties ended for No 1 link men.

Mr Nicholson said that, for some time, he had been considering the re-introduction of rounder trains, out of London to Ramsgate via Dover and back up to Victoria, with one engine and crew. He had in mind Stewarts Lane men going clockwise ie Victoria to Charing Cross via Ramsgate and Dover, the engine going into Ramsgate Loco for coal and water etc, while the Stewarts Lane men had their meal break. The B Arms men would start from Charing Cross and run to Ramsgate where they would have their meal break, while the engine was looked after by Ramsgate P&D men, then continue from Ramsgate to Victoria. The DMPS said that, in the past, rounder trains had worked well both for the company and the men, and that there was no reason why they should not do so again.

Charles Boarer, on behalf of Bricklayers Arms, asked if it would be possible for his men (and Stewarts Lane) to have a little more than the standard 20min preparation time. The DMPS said that he would try to see that the men got an hour, which he did. The B Arms Shed Master then said that he hoped that these rounder duties would have something decent on the front of them; a Schools would be ideal, since his depot had 18 and could get the best out of them. Again, the DMPS agreed quickly to this request and smiling, said that he had in mind to diagram a Schools, well coaled, to avoid the need for coaling at Ramsgate.

The summer rosters included a fair proportion of the rounder duties, shared between Stewarts Lane, Ramsgate and The Brick. The men in No 1 and No 2 links on reading through the roster sheets had to admit that the governor wasn't bad after all!

A Schools, well coaled, meant six tons on the tender, with a wall of large coal knobs, stacked carefully all round the tender top, giving plenty to re-make the fire after the Ramsgate P&D men had cleaned the fire. It was no secret that B Arms men preferred their own coal, which varied from No 2 Welsh to Yorkshire hards. The crews entered into the spirit of things and timekeeping on the trains was greatly improved as the weeks went by. B Arms was loath to let Stewarts Lane or Ramsgate get the better of them. Much of Stewarts Lane work was done by their King Arthurs on these trains, on which their men were more experienced. B Arms received one complaint regarding the running of one of the rounder trains. Running through Sevenoaks station one morning, a large knob of Yorkshire hard fell on to the platform, piercing the suitcase of a lady passenger waiting there. As the train roared through, the suitcase burst open and the unfortunate lady's change of under garments were rapidly whisked towards Sevenoaks tunnel! Luckily, the coal hit no one, or the consequences would have been serious. As it was, the lady was duly compensated and Bricklayers Arms received a strongly worded warning from the DMPS to ensure that coal was securely stacked. As the summer wore on, and ended, there were no further complaints regarding the running of the rounders.

While the holiday train running was good, since these

trains avoided rush hours, the running of the business trains came under criticism. A body of regular travellers, had formed themselves into The Season Ticket Holders Association and sent a letter to Waterloo regarding the regular late running of the 5.06 pm Cannon Street to Hastings (first stop Tunbridge Wells), a B Arms No 1 link duty. The letter was duly passed to the Shed Master concerned, for his comments. Mr Boarer knew of the constant checking of the train at Borough Market. Indeed, one of the top link drivers was so furious at the delay there, that he used to carry a hangman's noose in his pocket, which he used to hang from his extended arm, which was pointed directly at Borough Market signalbox! For the motive power office at Waterloo to trot out the well worn (though true) explanation of the fitting of steam trains into the world's busiest suburban electric service, would not pacify the gentlemen at all. The unusual step of allowing the spokesman of their association to ride on the footplate and see things over the driver's shoulder was then suggested.

No doubt lots were drawn as to who should act as observer and a few evenings later, accompanied by an inspector, a bowler-hatted city gentleman climbed into the cab of 30931 *Kings Wimbledon* to ride down on the 'terrible 5.06'. After the crew were introduced to the guest, they got on with the last minute preparations before the right away was given at 5.06. As if on cue, they were stopped dead at Borough Market for one minute; by the time they passed through No 3 platform at London Bridge, they were $2\frac{1}{2}$min down, which the guest duly noted. Driver Gillingham opened *Kings Wimbledon* fully into the first port and with her bridle rod on 30 per cent she galloped over the arches, passing New Cross (where the guest was firmly restrained from leaning out) at 5.14$\frac{3}{4}$, still $2\frac{1}{4}$min late. Driver Gillingham kept the cut-off at 30 per cent and being a large chimney Schools, she was barking just a bit. The fireman was firing as if his life depended on it and the engine was swaying, be it ever so gently. The guest, who had come on to the footplate as a hostile witness, was by Chislehurst, thoroughly enjoying himself, even though the train was, by then still 2min down. They swept through Sevenoaks, the lever back on 20 per cent, and according to the inspectors' watch the time was 5.36½. The descent through Sevenoaks tunnel was always exciting for the crew, and for the visitor the passage through both Polhill and Sevenoaks tunnels and the emergence into The Weald at 85mph was an experience never to be forgotten. *Kings Wimbledon* blew off steam vigorously when the regulator was shut for the rapidly approaching Tonbridge curve. They passed Tonbridge at 5.44½, still one minute late. With her ten-coach train, weighing 340 tons, 30931 attacked the climb to Tunbridge Wells, with her bridle rod on 40 per cent and full regulator—one always had to give her the lot up to the approaches to the goods yard. They stopped in the Wells at 5.55, still one minute late. The visitor thanked the crew for a thrilling and most enlightening experience and expressed the opinion that Waterloo should do something about the Borough Market delay which was the cause of late running and not, as they had first thought, a lack of effort on the part of the engine crew. By some strange chance delays at Borough Market became the exception rather than the rule after this visit.

If No 1 link were happier, so was the governor, but No 2 link men were complaining about the Midland type of 2–6–4T that they were given to run the 4.20 out of London Bridge because they suffered from injector trouble. Ever since this type of engine had come to the Southern, their injectors had given cause for complaint. A sudden brake application or the simple act of closing the regulator would cause the injector to blow-off, because the flow of water was interrupted. When this happened, the clack-valve (the self-seating non-return valve which allowed water to enter the boiler) failed to re-seat itself, steam from the boiler blew back through the clack and the injector became inoperable. To prevent the injector blowing off, drivers tended to run slowly into a station stop and of course, this caused late running.

Many of the Midland engines could be seen with steam wisping from the injector on the fireman's side, while the driver operated the injector on his side of the cab. Some men requested the use of the Southern's W class 2–6–4T, based at Hither Green, but since these engines were very similar to the ill-fated River class 2–6–4Ts, they were forbidden to run passenger trains; shades of the Riverhead accident of 1927, in which the stability of the River 2–6–4Ts was doubted, lingered on. Stewarts Lane was also complaining about the Midland tanks, which failed to run their 6.10 pm out of Victoria, for the same reasons. Enginemen and fitters alike could not understand how such a bad design of injector came to be adopted. Reading later literature one discovers that the London Midland Region had suffered from injector troubles for some time. In spite of the careful ministrations of Bert Wood and Charlie Richford and their band of fitters at The Brick, the Midland injectors were always a delicate piece of equipment to handle on an otherwise good design of engine.

By 1957, Bricklayers Arms had several Battle of Britain class Pacifics on its allocation, displacing the four King Arthurs. Several firemen took to wearing gloves when firing the Bulleid Pacifics, in order to place plenty of coal in the back corners of the oblique firebox. Singed wrists were an occupational hazard on this class of engine. At this time, too, many drivers were training on the new diesel-electric multiple unit trains (demus) which were to take over from the beloved Schools class on the Hastings run and by April, B Arms No 1 link had lost the 5.06 pm Cannon Street–Hastings to St Leonards shed.

A major operating disaster occurred in the early hours of 5 April when Cannon Street station signalbox caught fire; despite immediate action by signalmen and station staff—and the arrival of the fire brigade within 4min—the box was destroyed and the station put completely out of action. Fast steam services were diverted to Victoria and Charing Cross, while semi-fast trains which could be handled by rebuilt D1 and E1 4–4–0s, ran into and out of Holborn Viaduct (no four-coupled engines other than the D and E classes were allowed over Blackfriars bridge).

Remarkably it took only a month, with the installation of a temporary power lever frame, to get Cannon Street almost back to normal, but for St Leonards and B Arms men it was a sad day, for from 6 May two Cannon Street–Hastings trains were run by the ungainly looking six-car demu trains. The run-down of steam on the Hastings route was rapid indeed. for by 8 June 1958, the last Hastings train was steam hauled. Several B Arms Schools went to the Western Section, from whence they had come some 20 years before, and two of St Leonards Schools, which had been at that depot for almost 25 years, migrated to Bournemouth and Eastleigh. The net result of the Hastings dieselisation was a reduction in the number of spare locomotives at Bricklayers Arms.

Electrification of Kent Coast routes was on the way in 1957, but steam still had four years to go before the Tonbridge–Ashford–Dover route was converted. In order to give their firemen driving experience, it was the custom of some drivers in No 2 and No 1 links to change places with their mates. The drivers, while keeping a very close eye on signals, and the timetable, and giving their firemen expert tuition, were at the same time able to show that they could still fire to her, in spite of their advancing years.

Each driver had a favourite train on which to let his fire-man handle the regulator. In No 1 link it was generally the 8.25 am Charing Cross–Hastings, where the top link men relieved No 4 link men at London Bridge and were them-selves relieved at Tonbridge—a mere 30 miles on the shovel for the driver. As a matter of interest, the No 1 link men upon arrival at Tonbridge, walked to the loco depot and took a Schools to the up sidings, where they waited as spare engine for any up train that had engine trouble, until they returned to Charing Cross with the 1.57 pm from Tonbridge (due in Charing Cross at 2.55). In their first attempts to run the 8.25 down, the firemen used to tend to take it a little too easy as far as Grove Park where, on discovering that they had lost time, would open her up. When a certain fireman, whose name was Chopping, took over the regulator from his mate, Tom Merrett, he had no intention of losing time and according to his driver, passed Orpington 2min early. Poor old Tom, who was turned 60, kept the Schools on 220 all the way to Tonbridge, though his fireman did not hear another word from him until 1.57!

In No 2 link, a favourite change places turn was the 10.43 am from Brighton to Birkenhead, first stop, Redhill, where the B Arms men were relieved by Redhill men. The teddy bear 2–6–2T came off the train here and Redhill men, with an N class 2–6–0, coupled on at the back end as the train reversed and took the train on to Reading, where Great Western men and engine took over.

The quiet efficiency of the older driver is clearly illustrated by an occasion when Tom Merrett handled the firing on a teddy bear when running the Birkenhead one fine morning, many years ago. After coming down with the 5.08 am London Bridge–Brighton, via Horsham, which arrived in Brighton at 8.24 am, Tom and his fireman adjourned to a café for breakfast. At 10 am they relieved Brighton men in the station. Tom quietly said that he was to be fireman and started to make up the fire, while his mate made a tea-can full of hot, sweet tea. By the time the fireman returned to the engine the footplate had been washed down, fire made up, and Tom was sitting down, enjoying a cigarette. Tom had washed and had shut the bunker flap tight. At 10.35, he opened the damper wide, put a touch on the blower and sat down again. His mate was a little nervous, and studied a copy of the working timetable.

At 10.43, Tom shouted 'right away, driver' and sat down again. The fireman opened the regulator wide and with her train of seven coaches, the little tank engine trotted out of Brighton Station. Reverser back on 30 per cent, the fireman eased the regulator slightly and they were well and truly off. The driver (Merrett that is) was leaning out of his side window, apparently disinterested in the steam pressure gauge which hovered on 190lb (working pressure 200). Into the 492yd long Patcham tunnel, the engine was pulling nicely, and upon emerging into daylight again, the fireman took another look at the timetable and then at his watch.

His driver lit another cigarette and put the injector on, just in time to avoid the engine blowing off and then he sat down again, and resumed his gaze out of the side window. Through Clayton tunnel and Tom got up twice—once to pull the whistle cord at the entrance to the tunnel and once at the exit. The cut-off was back to 25 per cent, passing Haywards Heath at a good 65mph. The engine tore across the magnificent Ouse Valley viaduct, and Driver Merrett got up and crossed over to the driver's side of the cab, shouting to his fireman that all the bricks to build the viaduct were brought to the site by barges by a river which had by now, all but dried up; Tom then sat down again. Through the 1,141yd long Balcombe tunnel and into the morning sunshine again they went. The fireman took yet another look at the timetable and Tom shouted across 'Is that a good book?' The fireman looked at the steam pressure, 195lb, and wondered when his mate was going to start firing. Tom continued to look out of the window at the road ahead. Three Bridges flashed by as did Gatwick Airport and Racecourse stations. Horley was passed at 70mph and Driver Merrett shut off the injector. The fireman eased the regulator at Salfords and Tom got up and opened the firehole doors for the first time since leaving Brighton. There was slightly under a foot of fire, flat as a pancake all over the box, glowing brightly. The regulator was closed at Earlswood and the fireman braked the train gently since the Redhill distant was at caution, the outer home signal cleared and the fireman brought the train carefully into Redhill. The damper was closed and the boiler pressure was at 170, with just under half a glass of water. The fireman asked Tom how he had managed to judge the fire so well, having never fired a teddy bear before. The driver answered that he had never fired an Atlantic between

Victoria and Brighton, since they used to fill the firebox with lumps and he had treated the teddy bear the same way! The details of this run, incidentally, are clearly remembered by the fireman after all those years, since it was the first time I had driven a main line train!

The 'New' Shed at Bricklayers Arms, roofless since the blitz of 1940, could only be entered from the turntable. One afternoon some cleaners were working on a Brighton tank engine in the New Shed. The gang had half-cleaned the engine, and to allow the senior hand to finish cleaning the motion, it became necessary for the engine to be moved. One lad volunteered to go to the foreman's office to get the services of a driver or fireman to move the engine. Another lad, however, scorned this idea and said he was quite capable of moving the engine a few feet without the necessity of troubling the foreman. Moving an engine, he said, was simple and safe if one followed the rules the enginemen observed.

The lad climbed on to the footplate, while his colleagues watched. He put the vacuum ejector on and got 21 inches of vacuum. He opened the cylinder cocks, sounded the whistle, put the lever in forward gear and gently opened the regulator. The little engine moved off, but instead of stopping there and then, the lad decided to run on a little and stop a couple of yards from the edge of the turntable pit—the primary purpose of moving the engine, was of course, by now, forgotten. Approaching the pit, he released about 5in of vacuum, then more, and then he dropped the handle. It was now all too obvious to him—and his colleagues—that the little engine was not going to stop and he jumped from the cab as the engine nosed into the turntable pit, with a noise that echoed across the Old Shed, and rested on her buffers.

News travels fast and bad news even quicker. The running foreman was soon informed of the catastrophe, who in turn told the shed master that B Arms turntable was out of action necessitating engines turning at Ewer Street or Old Kent Road spur. The breakdown crane was in its usual place, next to the Carriage Shed wall and to get it close to the turntable,

No 5 road, Old Shed was cleared of engines, and the crane propelled through the shed. Someone had telephoned an evening newspaper and within a short time an attractive lady reporter arrived, with permission from Waterloo, to look at the scene and for a photographer to take a picture. When the young lady said she wished to interview the lad responsible, the governor shook his head and said to the effect that she had got her picture and that was all.

The culprit was eventually ushered into the shed master's office, the chargehand cleaner having warned the lad to expect the sack on the spot. The cleaner, though shaken, was genuinely puzzled as to why his footplate procedure had failed to work, and he faced his governor with the remark that he thought that the engine brakes were faulty. The governor explained that although the cleaner's footplate procedure was basically correct for enginemen, he knew only too well that cleaners were forbidden to be on the footplate at any time (all cleaning on the footplate was done by the fireman). Mr Boarer explained that had the lad used the Westinghouse compressed air brake equipment, the engine would have stopped, but the vacuum brake he so carefully used was only a blow-through to operate vacuum stock and did not apply the engine brake. The interview ended with the reminder that rules were made for safety and were not to be broken by 'children'. The cleaner waited for his dismissal, having proved that a little knowledge was indeed a dangerous thing. The dejected lad turned to leave, but the governor's last words rang in his ears, 'you had better tell the cleaner chargehand to find you the filthiest engine in this shed and don't go home until you have cleaned her or you will have another one to do, on your own tomorrow'. Rumour had it that the lad was hard at work within five minutes of leaving the governor's office! As to the engine, she was soon in the workshop and was back in service very soon afterwards, none the worse for her adventure.

That incident, though, was minor compared with events of 4 December 1957. The morning was foggy, though not unduly so, and gave no hint that it would thicken before dusk. It was to be a day that many hundreds of people would remember for many years to come. Trouble started around lunch time, when the Ramsgate spam diagrammed to work the 4.56 pm Cannon Street–Ramsgate via Ashford (the old 5 pm retimed to fit in with the new diesel services) was stopped for repairs when she came into B Arms depot. This put the running foreman on the spot since, because of the reduction in the stock of main line engines, he had no spare Schools, let alone a Pacific to stand-in for the stopped engine. He therefore worked the old pals act with Fred Pankhurst at Stewarts Lane. Panky was delighted to help his old depot out and shouted down the telephone that he had a spare spam, No 34066 *Spitfire*, only recently shopped. She was all ready, was a good 'un and what was more he would send her light to Rotherhithe Road with a pair of spare men, to pick up her empties.

Spitfire left Stewarts Lane Loco at 3.15 pm, after filling her tender tank to the brim. By the time she had threaded her way across London via Blackheath, the fog was thickening fast. In fact it took Driver Stewart 1½ hours to reach Rotherhithe Road where, upon arrival, they were relieved by Driver Charlie Jeffries and his mate, of B Arms. The four men agreed that it was going to be a really thick night. By the time *Spitfire* arrived at Cannon Street, at the head of her train, the time was 5.55. The Ramsgate men arrived at 6 pm and Driver Jeffries informed them that there was barely half a tank of water left—the fire having been made up for a 4.56 start. Without dampers the engine simply wasted water by blowing off steam many times. The Ramsgate driver duly informed the guard that he intended to stop at Sevenoaks for water, since there was no water column available at the head of their train. The train, totalling 258yd in length, consisted of 11 coaches, including a buffet car, with a seating capacity of 96 first class and 384 second class. The train was packed full, with standing passengers, so that the total was nearer 700.

Because of the fog, trains were completely out of turn,

though a formal fog service timetable was not in operation. It was not until 6.08 pm that *Spitfire* pulled out of Cannon Street, 72min late. In view of subsequent events it is important to put oneself into the position the driver was in; he was in charge of a damperless engine, with a low supply of water and was in a thick fog. Progress of the 4.56 was slow and the time allowed, under normal conditions to pass New Cross was exceeded by $3\frac{1}{2}$min as it was not until 6.18 that it passed that station. The following table shows the order of trains on the through line at St Johns that evening.

Train			Actual Depart time	Min late	Passing time St Johns booked	actual	Min late
5.05	(S)	CS–Has	5.43	38	5.13	6.00	47
5.16	(E)	CS–Orp	5.45	29	5.28	6.03	35
5.25	(D)	CX–Has	5.45	20	$5.37\frac{1}{2}$	6.08	$30\frac{1}{2}$
5.18	(E)	CX–Hay	5.48	30	5.34	6.11	37
4.56	(S)	CS–Ram	6.08	72	5.04	6.20	76

S–steam; E–electric; D–diesel; CS–Cannon St; CX–Charing Cross; Has–Hastings; Orp–Orpington; Hay–Hayes; Ram–Ramsgate

At Parks Bridge Junction signalbox, some misunderstanding arose on the description of the 5.25 Charing Cross to Hastings diesel multiple-unit. The signalman stopped this train as he thought it was the 5.18 electric to Hayes, which was booked to run via the Ladywell Loop (see sketch on page 138). Further confusion arose when the actual 5.18 stopped at signals behind the Hastings train. These events in no way reflected upon the signalman at Parks Bridge and when the true identity of the leading train (the 5.25) was established, the signals were cleared, and it departed. The 5.18, a 10-coach electric multiple-unit, weighing about 430 tons gross and carrying approximately 1,500 passengers, was now stopped on a rising gradient and the driver, J. Skilton, kept the brakes on. Travelling in the cab with him were Driver Jack Crane

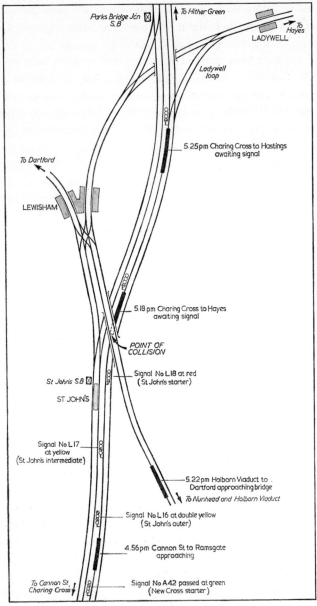

Fig 4 Track layout and position of trains moments before
the St Johns collision on 4 December 1957

and his fireman, who had been unable to get into the train to travel home as passengers because of the crowds. Driver Skilton, seeing them trying in vain to get in the train had asked them to ride with him in the cab to help him spot the signals. Behind them, the 4.56 had picked up a little speed. As was the custom, Fireman Hoare on *Spitfire* had observed the signals to New Cross, since they were situated on the inside of a right-hand curve, while his driver was on the left-hand side of the engine. The New Cross starter (signal A42) exhibited a green and after waiting until the engine had passed under the road bridge at the country end of New Cross station (which tended to blow back the fire) the fireman resumed firing since the next two signals, the St Johns outer (signal L16) and the St Johns intermediate (signal L17) were on the driver's side of the curve and normally easily visible from the driver's position.

Had the driver observed these two signals he would have seen that L16 was exhibiting a double-yellow and signal L17 one yellow, indicating that the St Johns starter, signal L18 was at danger. Fireman Hoare paused from his firing to see the aspect of the starter and shouted to his mate 'You've got a red', whereupon the driver smartly dropped the brake handle. Only 138yd ahead was the last coach of Driver Skilton's packed train.

Spitfire ploughed into the 5.18 at an estimated speed of 30mph. Severe telescoping of the coaches occurred and the body of the ninth coach was driven through the eighth. The engine remained on the track, but the tender was derailed and flung to the left taking the first coach with it, and demolishing one of the $14\frac{1}{2}$ ton steel columns that supported the overbridge which carried the Nunhead to Lewisham Loop line. About 350 tons of bridgework fell on to the leading coach of the 4.56, destroying it completely, and crushing half the second coach. The accident happened at 6.20 and at 6.22 ambulances were called from a nearby house. At that moment approaching the damaged bridge above was Motorman Corke in charge of the eight-car electric train from Holborn Viaduct to Dartford. Peering from his cab window through the fog, Motorman Corke suddenly observed a dip in the bridge ahead and promptly stopped his train, averting a further disaster.

Immediately after the collision, Driver Crane and his fireman, Nash, ran from the front cab of the 5.18 to the locomotive cab and found the *Spitfire* driver so badly shocked that they could get nothing coherent from him. Fireman Hoare of *Spitfire* was also shocked and badly injured and the two men smothered the fire in the engine with dirt and ballast to keep her quiet and prevent the risk of damage to the firebox, through shortage of water.

Shed Master Boarer was waiting at London Bridge to go home, when the public address system urged him to go to the telephone. He learned of the accident but to quote his own words he was totally unprepared for the scene of destruction he found upon arrival at St Johns. 'The wreck was a nightmare', he said, 'and the cries of the injured and the slowly dying will remain with me forever. Many passengers only slightly hurt or uninjured were too shocked to help in the urgent task of rescue. Many others, however, and the local residents were tearing at the wreckage with their bare hands. I summoned assistance from Control and cranes and equipment were sent from Stewarts Lane, Nine Elms, Ashford and my own depot at B Arms. Every available man arrived from Hither Green Loco to help. The doctors and nurses from Lewisham Hospital performed miracles every few minutes'. Such were Shed Master Boarer's first impressions. There were thoughts among the more senior men that it was this same train that had come to grief at Riverhead just 30 years before. By 10.30 pm all the injured had been released from the wreck; among them were two men from B Arms, travelling passenger to Ramsgate—Driver Dickinson, trapped in a compartment corner, covered in blood from a passenger who had been thrown up into the luggage rack above him, and bled to death. Another driver, Jim Burnett was also badly injured.

The press arrived and were refused permission to take

pictures until the human debris had been tidied up. All the newsmen respected this decision, except one photographer who wanted to show reality. He was surrounded by railwaymen who commented that his camera was expensive and delicate—he got their message, and waited. After 48 hours of continuous work the fallen bridge was shored up, the engine and undamaged coaches removed, and the men went home to sleep for 12 hours, though for many sleep eluded them for any length of time for some time afterwards.

The day after the accident, District Motive Power Superintendent Howard interviewed the 4.56 driver at his home, but like Driver Crane the previous day, he also was unable to get a coherent statement from him. At the ensuing enquiry, it was pointed out that *Spitfire* was in perfect working order on the day of the accident, since it had only run 3,444 miles since the last classified repair carried out in Eastleigh Works and had run a total of 357,391 miles from new. It was one of a number of Pacifics with the boiler pressure reduced to 250lb/sq in. Like all the Bulleid Pacifics, it had a steam brake on the engine wheels and vacuum on the tender wheels, all of which were subsequently tested, as were the remaining train vehicles, and found to be in perfect working order.

The previous steam train to pass St Johns was the 5.05 pm Cannon Street to Hastings, and St Leonards Fireman Emery, said he had a good fire on leaving Cannon Street but because of the poor visibility gave Driver F. Frewn, all his attention by spotting signals. When the fireman of the 4.56 was asked why he resumed firing instead of continuing to help his driver to observe signals, he replied that he did not realise just how thick the fog was and since signal A42 was a green and the next two signals normally were in easy view of his driver, he started to build up his fire in preparation for the climb to Knockholt. He noticed that his driver did not cross the footplate at any time and naturally assumed that he had observed signals L16 and L17.

When the 4.56 driver was asked why he did not reduce speed when, from his knowledge of the road, he must have realised that he had missed two signals, the driver's reply indicated that since he had never been stopped at St Johns before he assumed he would not be stopped there then. At the subsequent trial, where the driver was charged with the manslaughter of the guard of the 5.18 train, this reply caused some doubt in the minds of the jury and a retrial was ordered. When it opened, the prosecution stated that it had no evidence to offer and the driver was acquitted in view of his physical and mental state.

Newspapers naturally demanded to know what was wrong with British Railways as a whole and the Southern Region in particular. They did not do their homework, which the chief inspecting officer of railways most certainly did, before he published his official report. The four tracks between New Cross and St Johns, were one of the busiest sections of railway line in the world, carrying about 990 passenger trains in 24 hours. At the height of the evening home-going traffic, about 81 trains passed through St Johns in one hour. No fatal accident had occurred since the four-aspect colour-light signals superseded semaphore signals in 1929. In fact, the last recorded fatal accident at St Johns was on 21 March 1890, when three passengers were killed and 20 injured in a collision during fog.

Normal services were resumed on the main and local lines on 12 December, but the Nunhead line was not reopened until 13 January 1958. The bridge was rebuilt with army trestles, at first as a temporary measure, but today regarded as permanent. The 4.56 driver was given a job in the stores at his home depot, but he could not bear to face them and retired to the West Country, where he died, a broken man. How many of us have, at some time, neglected to check something that should be checked, yet since it has never needed checking before, we have failed to do so? A lapse of attention for just 60 seconds was the cause of the St Johns accident.

9

Steam bows out

To many men on the Southern, it seemed strange that for a railway that had begun to oust steam as early as the 1920s, so many locomotives were built in the late 1940s and early 1950s. The original policy of Southern management was to run steam until the complete electrification of the system was possible; intermediate dieselisation was primarily the decision of the British Railways Board much later on. Economy in steam operation had for long been the watchword on the Southern; as an example the Westerham branch, with its two-coach pull-and-push train operated by Tonbridge men, continued to puff up and down its three station line. The local trains from Sevenoaks to Tonbridge, with their H class 0–4–4 tanks and three birdcage coaches had hardly changed since South Eastern & Chatham days around the first world war.

From the city, the 7.07 am, from Holborn Viaduct to Ramsgate via London Bridge and Dartford, continued to take 3hr 11min to reach Ramsgate, but as 1958 arrived, this train started out of Cannon Street and so ended an era. In No 6 link, there was still an ex-New Cross turn which provided a steam train service from New Cross Gate station to London Bridge, though few enthusiasts used this rare service since it left New Cross Gate at 4.30 am! This duty was run by an E5 radial to the very end; the train formed the 5.08 am to Horsham.

For No 2 link men the return trip from running the 6.18 pm down, was the 9.40 pm from Ashford to Holborn Viaduct via Maidstone East, all stations to Bromley South, then fast to Elephant & Castle, where B Arms men were relieved by Stewarts Lane men at 11.50 pm. Also in No 2 link, the return trip from running the 7.34 pm Charing Cross–Dover, was the 11 pm fast freight from Ashford, nonstop to Paddock Wood—a run originally assigned for an N class 2–6–0 when they were brand new engines.

One of the toughest night's work, however, was in No 4 link—or to be correct, morning's work, since the crew signed on at 12.15 am. They prepared a WD 2–8–0 then ran light to Sorting Sidings at 1.15 am, to work the heavy 1.40 am B Arms to Paddock Wood and Tonbridge Yard via Maidstone East. They generally used to arrive in Tonbridge Loco at around 4.30 am, where they would dispose of the engine (clean the fire, empty the smokebox, rake out the ash-pan and take on coal and water), a good hour's hard, hot work. After a short meal break, they then prepared a German (L class 4–4–0) and at 6.50 am took a train of empty coaches to Edenbridge, on the Old Road. From here they ran the 7.27 am passenger train to London Bridge via Oxted, one of the few trains which used the Crowhurst spur between Edenbridge (SEC) and Oxted. This train called at all stations to East Croydon, and was then fast to London Bridge, due in at 8.20. Often no relief was available, so the crew then ran the 8.40 empties to New Cross Gate, then ran light to join the long line of engines waiting at B Arms Loco for coal. By this time, having prepared two engines and disposed of one, the fireman was usually requested to put the German away, finishing duty about 11 am. After a week of that duty—it ran Monday to Saturday, since most offices then worked on Saturday mornings—the crew had had enough. They had started the week on overnight Sunday/Monday at 2 am, as required!

In contrast with the long South Eastern Section duties, the inherited Central Section duties, were shorter in hours, though still busy. To work the 8.36 am London Bridge to Brighton the enginemen signed on at 6.30 am and prepared their engine, an I3 4–4–2T or an SEC 4–4–0 but latterly a teddy bear 2–6–2T. They were relieved in Brighton Loco and then worked back to Victoria, where again, on arrival, they were relieved. To work the 3.23 am London Bridge to Brighton paper train, the men signed on at 2.30, engine seen away, to be out of the depot by 2.45 and run light to London Bridge. Over the years the engines had changed from an LBSCR B4X 'Grey Lady' 4–4–0 to a River class 2–6–4 tank, which ran the train quite well until they were withdrawn from service in 1927, and then when the main line electrification to Brighton displaced them, the beautiful Atlantics took over. By 1948 this duty was allocated to a Schools. In the early 1950s it became a West Country duty. On arrival in Brighton at 4.40 am, the pair took the engine into the cramped Brighton Loco, where the B Arms men would put her away. They returned with the fish train to London Bridge at 5.30. It was rumoured that the fish was then sold at Billingsgate Market and went back to Brighton on the 8.36 down! All fish traffic was dealt with at No 10 platform at London Bridge, which smelled perpetually like a fishmonger's shop! Drivers and motormen entering this platform, used to do so with great care as the rails were always very slippery. Many an unwary motorman has felt the wheels of his train pick up and slide when running in to that platform and had some anxious moments. One or two did touch the buffer stops!

Earlier I described the duty covering the 5.08 am via Horsham, returning in the summer months with the Birkenhead. In winter, this train did not run and the No 2 link men used to ride home 'on the cushions' as passengers or more often than not, back in the motorman's cab of a fast electric to Victoria. After firing all stations from Peckham Rye to Brighton via Horsham and Steyning, the fireman would have a go on a 6PUL/6PAN 12-car electric train, and by moving one handle have 3,600 horse power to provide the motive power instead of a firing shovel.

One rare occasions, the Brighton foreman would make himself unpopular with the visiting enginemen by having an engine which needed to be returned to the London area.

Passage for the light engine was arranged behind the hourly electric non-stop to London, and some fine running then ensued. One morning, Brighton Loco had a C2X o-6-o, belonging to B Arms, and an ex-New Cross man, Driver Ted Jakes, ran her so fast that he was checked outside Three Bridges, as he was overhauling the electric! Driver Jakes also loved the Atlantics and used to reckon that the South Eastern men were scared of them. It was true that the Atlantic had a high footplate, with wheels 6ft 7½in in diameter. They had a roomy footplate, with the driver seated up on a stage above the general level of the rest of the footplate, giving him a wide field of view and, no doubt to some of the drivers, the feeling of 'a king on a throne'. The exhaust injector was nowhere near as good as that on a Schools; to a fireman—a South Eastern one that is—it was the tip-flap firehole door that made these fine engines unpopular.

It was surprising how many of the older engines hung on until electrification, including many of the SEC 4-4-os and the King Arthur 4-6-os. Many men at The Brick referred to the King Arthurs as 'one legged', because of the distinctive sound made by an Arthur at speed. On paper, they were superior to a Schools in tractive effort, but in practice a Schools could see an Arthur off, any time of day or night. The four B Arms Arthurs, 794 *Sir Ector de Maris*, 795 *Sir Dinadan*, 798 *Sir Hectimere* and 799 *Sir Ironside,* were paired with small tenders and were originally designed for the Central Section.

Regular duties for the B Arms King Arthurs included the 7.34 pm Charing Cross–Dover and the 10.00 am Ewer Street to Dover Marine ferry vans. The latter was a Q train and only ran when required. It was a rostered duty in No 6 link and when it did not run, the men were in the yard. Most firemen found this train an easy introduction to running a train down the main line. Signing on at 7.00 am, they prepared the Arthur and ran light to Ewer Street, where they waited until the rush hour traffic was over. The fire was made up and allowed to burn through slowly, so that by the time 10 am arrived, it was just right. The load was usually 20 Continental long-wheelbase four-wheeled vans. If for any reason the train did not get the road at 10 am, instead of being routed down the main line via Orpington, it was often sent over the mountains via Maidstone East. The fireman was instructed to fire seven shovelfuls at a time, to keep a sloping fire, and only to use the half-flap. At a steady 40mph the Arthur would chug along and, when Dover Marine was reached, it was light to Dover Loco, put her away, then home passenger. Many firemen (myself included) used to ride back to Victoria on the footplate of an engine hauling a boat train, and when an Arthur was at the head of one of these heavily-loaded trains—12 and a van—one saw just how an Arthur had to be flogged to keep time. The visiting engineman would sometimes be 'assistant fireman' and by Ashford have the shovel all to himself; before Tonbridge was passed, the B Arms man would wish he had stayed in the train, with his driver, who would often refresh himself in the refreshment car with cold beer; at Victoria he would tell his fireman what a nice run back it was, looking at the countryside over a glass of cool, Kentish ale.

On the night of 26/27 October 1959, a severe gale blew across Kent. The 2.45 am light engine from Bricklayers Arms —Ashford via Hither Green and Maidstone East—was in the care of Driver George King. Approaching Bearsted, the driver saw an obstruction on the line and found a large tree had been blown down across both the up and down lines. Although he and his fireman tried to move it, they could not, so they left a red light on the obstruction and Driver King then hurried to Bearsted signalbox. He found it closed, but not for long for King opened the box and placed all signals at danger in time to stop an up ferry van train from Dover Marine. He then telephoned Maidstone East station and Control at Orpington. On the occasion of his 45 years in railway service, he received the customary gold watch plus a cheque for his vigilance and prompt action.

With the electrification completed on the Chatham line to

Ramsgate and Dover in 1959 withdrawals of steam locomotives increased in pace. Already some had gone when
diesel locomotives were borrowed from other regions pending
electrification. By the end of 1959, two H class tanks (31327
and 31329) had been withdrawn, together with an L class
4–4–0, No 31770. By February 1960, B Arms lost three of
the L1s, 31785, 31788 and 31784, three C2X 0–6–0s, 32442,
32551 and 32554, followed in March by a C class 0–6–0,
31033. By January 1961, Schools class No 30919 and 30932
were withdrawn for scrapping, together with L1, 31787, and
B Arms best King Arthur, 30799 *Sir Ironside* was scrapped
one month later. B Arms men were pleased though to know
that their Schools 4–4–0s continued in service in the South
Western Division until December 1962. Happily, three were
spared the cutters torch; BR preserved No 30925 *Cheltenham*,
30926 *Repton* went to Steamtown, USA and 30928 *Stowe*,
after being at Beaulieu Abbey, has now gone to another home
at Cranmore in Somerset.

Shed Master Boarer started to hand out redundancy notices
in early 1962. Attention was drawn to the vacancy list, for
drivers' vacancies at Hither Green or to the new electric
stabling point at Grove Park sidings, where not so long before
many had struggled to keep the spams quiet while waiting
time on the down, round, and back turns. Foreman George
Russell left B Arms to join the staff of the line manager's
office, SE Division and between May and June of 1962, 19
B Arms drivers transferred to Grove Park Depot as electric
drivers, and two as leading drivers. Nearly 70 men elected
to go to Hither Green and eight to Margate Depot, now
Ramsgate.

By June 1962 the electrics were in full swing on the
Tonbridge and Dover main line and all steam working in
the South Eastern and Central Divisions had finished. Many
of the lightly-used branches had been closed; some, as for
example the Oxted and Tonbridge–Hastings routes had been
dieselised with multiple-units, and a few, like the Maidstone
West branch from Paddock Wood, had been electrified.

Multiple-unit trains worked most passenger services including the boat trains, while freight and parcels trains were turned over to diesel or electric locomotives, or to a then new brand of locomotive, the electro-diesel, which could run off the third rail as an electric, but from a small diesel power plant to power the motors on non-electrified lines and sidings.

The men at B Arms held a collection for the shed master, who was transferring to the line manager's office. Men who had been at B Arms for 30 years, remembered the last collection held for a governor in the early 1930s. The total amount of money collected then was a token of their affection for him— one shilling and elevenpence-halfpenny—call it 10p! However the whip round for the first and last shed master of Bricklayers Arms was sufficient for a dinner with enough over to present him with a greenhouse, which stands today in the garden of his Newhaven home.

The changeover from steam to electric and diesel duties was easy for most men, but very hard for the older men, many of whom had served the pre-grouping SECR and LBSCR companies, the Southern Railway and British Railways as engine drivers and firemen. Some, could not get used to joining an electric roster where the most junior and senior drivers covered the same duties on the roster for there had never been such a thing as links in electric sheds. In order to get as much work out of an electric train driver without paying him mileage, all electric duties tend to be split. Thus a driver can work a main line train from Charing Cross to Sevenoaks, a local from Sevenoaks to Holborn, back to Sevenoaks, then relieve on a main line as far as Tonbridge and so on.

The thing that steam drivers missed most was the companionship of the engine cab and the way passengers now ignored them at the end of a run. On steam trains, it was unusual if at least one passenger did not thank the driver for a good run. Few people seemed interested in the cab of an electric train, whereas there was always somebody hanging about a steam locomotive cab, hoping to be invited up to look round.

The electric-train driver, has at his command, the equivalent power of three Schools class 4–4–0s on his 12-coach
train, but he has less time in which to cover the old steam
routes. For example, a boat train from Victoria to Dover used
to be allowed 100min—now it is only 80, so that the work of
watching the road is that much harder, although the driver
has a clearer view. Moreover, the driver is helped with the
automatic warning system which gives an audible warning
of signal aspects in the cab.

So ended the steam era on the South Eastern Section.
B Arms depot was demolished, and the weeds now grow where
the cleaners used to staple the breakdown crew's clothing to
the wall. There is still a black patch, where the coal stage
used to be, and perhaps on certain nights one can stand on
Dunton Road bridge and hear a ghostly West Country,
Schools or Stirling 0–6–0 whistle for the road.

One thing is certain: through the efforts and enterprise of
various societies throughout the country, steam will be with
us for many years yet. The few full-time enginemen and a
host of volunteers will continue to handle the regulator and
swing the shovel, so that young and old can still ride behind
steam, smell the hot oil and engine smoke and hear and see
again, or maybe for the first time, that sound and sight that
has no equal—a steam locomotive hard at work.

Index